ARRIVAL PRESS

Wild About Animals

Edited by Tim Sharp

Wild About Animals

EDITED BY TIM SHARP

First published in Great Britain in 1997 by

ARRIVAL PRESS
1-2 Wainman Road, Woodston,
Peterborough, PE2 7BU
Telephone (01733) 230762

All Rights Reserved

© *Copyright Contributors 1997*

HB ISBN 1 85786 651 7
SB ISBN 1 85786 646 0

Foreword

Everybody loves animals, whether they are green and scaly or the more conventional cute and cuddly. There is something that appeals to our spirit which makes us like and be fascinated by them.

I'm sure everyone has a tale to tell of some kind of animal or pet they have seen around.

The authors of the poems contained within *Wild About Animals* share their experiences, whether they are happy or sad, about pets past and present.

I am sure you will enjoy this inspirational collection of verse and take comfort in its pages.

Tim Sharp
Editor

Contents

It's A Pup's Life	Rita Bradshaw	14
The Tiger	Jenny Adams	15
Firkin	Anne Sharman	16
Drawing A Guinea Pig	P S Joll	17
The Female Of The Species	Doug Thomas	18
Our Grand-Dog	Anne Baker	19
Second Look	Mary Care	20
Heaven-Sent!	Mary Skelton	21
Let's Love All Animals	Albert Moses	22
The Harvest Mouse	Simon J Oksien	23
The Greyhound	C E Threader	24
The Little Grey Cock	Olive Torkington	26
A Doggy Tale	Lynda Paterson	27
Down The Years	Doreen Mason	28
I Am A Little Pussy Cat And Only One Pound Fifty	Michael Lyons	30
A Feathered Thought	Anne Kerr	32
I Am Just A Seal	Jeff D Hibbard	33
Secretive Cats	Jennifer A Hayes	34
The Bleak Mid-Winter	M Brindley	35
Who's A Clever Boy	S Nicolaou	36
The Day I Finished With My Girlfriend	Lawrence Richards	37
Mitzy	Iris Simmonds	38
Little Koe	Janet Boulton	39
Felix	Helen Marie Cairns	40
Meg	Iris Covell	41
A Dog Called 'Suzi'	Betty Bramma	42
Trail Of Tears	Spike	43
From Hutch To Heaven	Jean Castle	44
Sabre	Stephanie Churchill	45
You Love Me	R Medland	46
Flossie	Wm Chapman	47
Pirate Whalers	Luciene Azique	48
Topsy	T Betty Chadwick	50

Sinead Called Her Connie		Robert E Fairclough	51
Cruel Fool		Josephine McGaughran	52
The Camel And The Otter		James Cuin	53
Sheba		Joan Walker	54
The Vanishing Weersigonn		Glenn R Lumb	55
Pavy		Iris Jones	56
I Am The Tiger		Hilary Beevers	57
It's A Dog's Life		Alison Hawtin-Dumbrava	58
In My Heart		Jo Upton	59
Wesley The Westie Update		Eileen M Ward	60
Waiting To Be Chosen		Mary E Beale	61
A Dog And His Problem		Jacqueline Claire Davies	62
Squirrel (Nipper) Remembered		Mary Ethridge	64
Caged Beast		Paul Birkitt	65
Animal Love		Doris Hoole	66
Kitten Of My Dreams		Miran McEntee	67
Wee Mac		Jean Hendrie	68
My Budgies		Christine Kowalkowski	69
Warning! Budgie On The Loose		Irene Witte	70
Dolphins		K Brown	71
Pride Of Love		David Bridgewater	72
Snout In The Trough		Chris Bailey	73
Cat Moods		Nancy Leeson	74
Ringo		Dawn-Marie Gibbons	75
Killer On The Couch		Chris Birkitt	76
Amy		Alyson Mountjoy	77
Nikki The Mischievous Cat		Alastair Buchanan	78
Danny		Mandy Biro	79
Here To Stay		Pauline Jones	80
Friendly		David Galvin	81
Us And Them		Claire Shellis	82
Shelley		Sara Newby	84
No Other		Glennis Horne	85
Tadsor Arabian Stud		Margaret Lord	86
Kelly		Joan Hands	87
Chicko		Vivienne Joyce	88

Title	Author	Page
A Hymn For Creatures Great And Small	Linda J Bodicoat	89
A Tree Full Of Birds	Malcolm Lisle	90
Sanctuary At 'Freshfields'	Mary Marriott	91
Lop Ears	Margaret Brazier	92
The Heart-Broken Chicken	Karen Jones	93
Old Jenny	Marlene S Browne	94
Educated Dog	Sally Quinn	95
To A Cat	I McKenzie-Young	96
Triple Joy	Betty Robertson	97
Suzie And Cracker	Cynthia Shum	98
Sadie	Fiona Ballantine	99
My Friend	Rachel Hudson	100
Our Pets	Pamela Eckhardt	101
On Walking The Dog	Bryan Holden	102
A Friend For Life	June Stokes	103
The Barn Owl	Val Reed	104
Don't Panic . . .?	Jenny Prescott	105
Ants	Jessie Knox	106
Water Queen In My House	Amita Saxena	107
The Family Feline	Sara Russell	108
Tara	Ruth Edna Bailey	110
My Dog Chips	Rosa Butterworth	111
Ode To Sally	Betty Robertson	112
Babe, My Budgie	Marjorie Horgan	114
The Hedgehog	Margaret Jackson	115
Animal Crazy?	Jo Sutherland	116
To Samson (1992-1996)	Olivia Kennedy	117
Poppy Day	Bob Darvell	118
If I Were	E Sturdy	119
Longing	Megan Hughes	120
Brock's A 'Second'?	Eileen M Lodge	121
Ballad To A Pig	Joan Richardson	122
Tessa	Frances Cook	123
Those Mucky Geese	Marilyn K Hambly	124
Alice	L T Coleman	125
Instincts	Michael Avery	126
To Joker	C L Pearson	127

Title	Author	Page
Animal Cruelty	Beverley Wilson	128
My Special Friend	Emma Gale	129
A Visit With Libby	Jean McGovern	130
Lucky	David A Garrett	132
My Special Friend	J W Whitehead	133
My Brave Wally	Ann G Wallace	134
Where?	Lisa Dilloway	135
Bosun	Sue Lowe	136
The Old Barn Cat	Olive Torkington	138
Free Bird	Bernadette O'Reilly	139
My Dog Is Waiting	Caroline Merrington	140
The Horse	Brian P Carroll	141
An Unconditional Love	Shirley Ann Lewis	142
Jack	Lynda Blagg	143
Dino	Paula Wright	144
My Garden	J M James	145
Sally (Loyal Friend)...	Sandra Seed	146
A Dedication To Burty	L P Smith-Warren	147
Sam	J M Stoles	148
Wise Owls	Polly Pullar	149
Chloe	Pam Bowyer	150
In Memory Of Misty	Rosie Hart	151
Companions, Lost	Etelka Marcel	152
Scamp	Edna Ridge	154
My Mum	J Munday	155
Begging Your Pardon	Adrian Cooper	156
A Hedgehog's Fear	Kim Adams	158
Fatal Attraction	Frances Le Gray	159
The Scorpion	Monica F James	160
The Pekingese	Angela Kellie	161
Our Dumb Friend	Clare Graham	162
Gem	Margherita Osborne	163
The Dinner Date	Julie D Ashton	164
Twinkle	Phyl Clarkson	165
Tiger	Nancy Webster	166

The Poems

It's A Pup's Life

I've had a million things to do
On this sunny summer's day.
First I had to chase the cat
Whilst pretending it was play.

Then I had my breakfast
Which was followed by a bone.
It took me ages to bury it
In a strictly dog-free zone.

And then I had to have a nap,
It's tiring, all this fun.
Human's just don't realise
The stress till work is done.

I had to inspect the garden next -
Those cats get everywhere.
The one next door is cheeky,
It goes with the red hair.

The walk was fun, but really -
Do they have to jog that way?
It makes me quite embarrassed
About what other dogs will say.

I slept the afternoon away,
It really was so hot.
The humans did the gardening,
They got through quite a lot.

We had a barbecue for dinner
And I got loads and loads.
The birds ate all the leftovers,
They came round in their droves.

Another walk, then bedtime -
It's exhausting keeping up.
Don't they realise that after all
I'm just a mongrel pup?

Rita Bradshaw

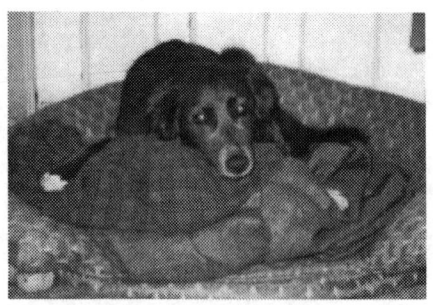

The Tiger

The tiger roams so wild and free among the grass and trees,
He looks for danger nearby and stares at what he sees.
The people gather round the enclosure to observe this amazing creature,
The tiger looks back calmly and reveals his great feature.
The keeper comes by at two o'clock to feed the tiger his meat,
He walks over calmly and then viciously takes the treat.
Closing time at the zoo was drawing near,
The tiger walked swiftly to his den without fear.
The keeper passed the enclosure again and was greeted with an almighty roar,
The tiger wanted freedom but he couldn't have that anymore.
He was in the zoo for years to stay,
While people watched his moves day by day.

Jenny Adams (16)

Firkin

A ball of fur, grey and white,
With tiny needle teeth to bite.
Dashing here and rushing there,
Without a solitary care.
She leaps out upon your feet,
Then eats until she is replete.
In a slipper playing hide and seek;
Suddenly taking off with a squeak.
Who is it, making out heads spin?
Our neighbour's kitten called Firkin.

Anne Sharman

DRAWING A GUINEA PIG

She sits neatly, delicately,
her four feet,
one black, three saffron,
collected underneath her
ready for saltation:
alert, bright-eyed,
gleaming-whiskered,
tortoiseshell.

Bicoloured.
A chocolate digestive biscuit.
Conjunct ellipses:
fine-held head curves over
her soft warm glossy oval rippled body.

P S Joll

The Female Of The Species

My lady came in search of tea
  Head aloft, imperiously,
She looked around with some distaste
  At all the sloth and lack of haste

Her fur was from the upper class,
  It shone like sheets of purest glass
And when she smiled her teeth were white,
  Anticipating that first bite

She wandered through an open door
  And stretched her legs upon the floor,
An empty chair, with cushions deep,
  Persuaded her to fall asleep

She dreamed of roaming round a house,
  Inhabited by a large mouse,
Her ears twitched and her fur arose,
  Then daintily she touched her nose

She woke up in an awful fright
  And stretched her head to its full height,
Then knocking over one small chair,
  She sat and gave her 'fed-up' stare

Surely her meal was ready now
  And she let out one long meow,
Then jumped upon the table top
  With one hungry but graceful hop

And there it was the caviar,
  Straight from her very special jar,
Fit for a charming lady's plate,
  In spite of being very late

Doug Thomas

Our Grand-Dog

Dillon always came to meet us, with dad's slippers at the door.
When he was a puppy, the same ones he would gnaw.
He'd put his head upon my lap, his brown eyes made a plea.
He'd say without so many words, 'I think it's time for tea.'

When our grandsons came along, he watched and played with care.
He wasn't selfish either, with them his toys he shared.
Fifteen years devotion and affection, both he gave.
A very special grand-dog, whose memory won't fade.

He had a gentle nature, with warm and winning ways.
We loved him and now grieve for him, now he is in his grave.
Beneath the daffodils he lies, a peaceful quiet place.
I only need to close my eyes to see his trusting face.

Our lives - richer by far he made, our love will never cease.
A wooden cross now bears his name.
Dillon
R.I.P

Anne Baker

Second Look

I dared to creep closer,
surprised he didn't move,
a small white ball of fluff
by the side of the field.

He trembled like a leaf,
too frail to run and skip,
the little lamb crouched low,
so alone and afraid.

Abandoned by the flock,
his soft white downy coat
tried hard to keep him warm
in the short dewy grass.

But where was his mother,
why had she left him there,
didn't she know his need
for comfort of her warmth?

Life was very cruel
when little legs were weak;
if only he could skip
with the rest of the lambs.

I sadly walked away
and still he didn't move,
but when I turned I saw
his mother tending him.

Mary Care

HEAVEN-SENT!

The animal world
is everywhere
in countries far and wide,
their comfort lies
where they're most at ease
in their natural habitat.

It's wrong for Man
to hunt them
or cruelly move them on,
God gave a natural shelter
to every living thing.

Likewise our domestic pets
their birthright should be blessed,
with loving care in home-surrounds
to bring all-round happiness.

Such a faithful friend
the family dog -
and a cat will purr content,
a convivial background for the home,
and truly -
Heaven-sent!

Mary Skelton

LET'S LOVE ALL ANIMALS

Animals on this earth are living with us
and are not here to fight against us
They, a balance to the ecology provide
we must try and understand their pride

They look to man for protection
that is their natural attraction
We should observe them in the wild
they have simply nothing to hide

Their beautiful fur is for their protection
and certainly not for our collection
God gave them the fur to fit their body
and not to be torn away from their body

Would we like to be killed for our skin?
Then why are we committing this sin?
We must learn to live and let live
and our love and protection to them give

We could learn from the love of our pets
they give us their company and love us lots
Look into their eyes and we will see
their love for all of us is clear as can be

So loving and faithful
and ever so grateful
They wag their tail or purr in appreciation
and cuddle up to you for love and affirmation

Isn't it such a treat to hear their heart beat
as they warm up to us and feel our body heat
That is real comforting love
reminding us to give them our eternal love.

Albert Moses

The Harvest Mouse

A small and tiny
puff of life
the harvest mouse
sees danger and strife
as he climbs the corn
up to the ears
and makes his nest
where babes are born
he's camouflaged
with tawny coat
creamy markings
upon his throat
his little paws
to hold a seed
feeds his young
in time of need
save them do
at harvest time
a safe place
for to recline
and see them through
the winter harsh
these small and clever
little mites
save, help and guard
their very right

Simon J Oksien

The Greyhound

This dog that is fleet of foot
Is after the quarry when he is put

Of monarchs the dog is prized
And others race him for a prize

Greeks and Romans knew of him
About him they make a din

Full of praise by all who have
                a dog such as him
Praises and praises some would sing hymns
But look at him standing there
Elegance beyond compare

In body neat and slender
Turn at speed a real bender

Eyes so bright clear and true
What dog has this very few

Legs of steel made of springs
When he runs he has his fling

But when after a hare in the field
He has but one spot and won't yield

People have some for pets
Seldom they go to the vets

In kennels they abound
For dog racing they are found

Money is on their backs
Treated like sacks

Food and water they are given
For affection they are striven

Years of service is their lot
A life of luxury theirs is not

In the box out to train
Even when it is rain

Days of warm and cold
Out they go when they are told

So their life takes its toll
Sooner than others they are old

What becomes of them in the end
Now they are over the hill and round the bend

Some sad to say are not there today
Others find homes and there's no pay

People see these majestic creatures
And not their special features

But to walk them takes a time
More so when they are in their prime

Miles and miles is their track
You acts like on a rack

See a cat covered in fur
Cat sees dog and doesn't purr

The hair is up and on the tail
If dog went it wouldn't fail

But dog is held by the lead
Cat is safe that's all we need

Now as the days come to an end
A racing dog is a real friend

C E Threader

The Little Grey Cock

He was only a little grey bantam cock,
Ten a penny the man said, aiming a kick at his head.
Have him if you can catch him or he'll soon be dead.
Two long hours it took me to catch that little bird,
The man said I could have him and he kept his word.
I placed him in my hen-pen with seven great big hens,
He bobbed and danced and spread his wings, and crowed
and did all sorts of things.
He pecked and clucked and scratched about,
He was a good one at pulling worms out,
Not for himself, but for the seven fat wives,
The little grey cock has got a new life.

Olive Torkington

A Doggy Tale

My name is Pepsi Paterson
I'm as quiet as a mouse,
I don't like cats and dogs and birds
coming near my house.

I'm only a little dog -
a pretty one at that,
the last thing I want near my food
is a cheeky, pesky cat!

One day I had a nasty shock -
this creature came to stay
I look at it - it was a cat,
you can imagine my dismay!

It's only a little ball of fluff,
but had sharp teeth and claws.
My owners named him Chocolate Chip,
I would have named him *Jaws!*

He ate my food, he chewed my toys,
he pushed me from my bed.
He bullied me, and teas-ed me,
and pounced upon my head.

I've growled at him, and told him off,
and made some rules today.
If he doesn't heed my words
I've told him he can't stay.

He's grown a bit, and settled down,
and rubs his head on mine,
He purrs to me and tells me things,
Now we're doing just fine.

Lynda Paterson

Down The Years

It started with lovely boy Recco
Then Linda, a pretty blue roan.
They were happy and loving and giving
And such a joy to own.

Then came along white, woolly Kim
And Linda number two
Her coat was so soft and glossy
And such a lovely hue.

Next there came Rip the tearaway
So aptly named was he
He hung around with a bad lot
And a long life was not to be!

What can I say about Rusty?
So loving, devoted and kind
He was left with us by his owner
Who walked on and ne'er looked behind.

Next there came the poodles
Six altogether so far
Recco two and little Sam
And big Sam, now he was a star.

And then my dear little Bonnie
Who was always so close to my heart
After eighteen years of devotion
Tears fell when we had to part.

But we've still got dear old Anna
Though her limbs are creaky and slow
And as for that little tyke Georgie
Oh! Such a delight to know.

I look back down the years with nostalgia
To those that have come and gone
Such love, such devotion is priceless
Worth more than a golden crown.

Doreen Mason

I Am A Little Pussy Cat And Only One Pound Fifty

Hi, I'm a little pussy cat
I'm only one pound fifty
'A cute little ball of fluff,' you say?
Well, isn't that just lovely
you're in for a little shock, dummy
Hello domestic bliss
say goodbye to the runners up?
What do you think this is?
Thanks for nothing, losers
you'll find yourself a home
and by the way, you up there
it had better be warm!

So this is home, not bad
it's really pretty cool
not a bad little kitchen
and I love the living room
so that must be the garden
for those lazy summer days
I'll check it out later,
but first, this place.
What's on the menu?
I might as well taste it
but whether I like it or not
is up to me let's face it!

They had better not be noisy
while I'm taking forty winks
I might be cute, but hey!
This one needs time to think
I like to play,
but all that over-exertion's overrated
all of that's for stupid dogs

not for this one, matey!
The neighbours better measure up
that goes for the owners too
if they give me any hassle
I'll give them something too!

I think I'm going to like it here
so I've decided to stay
this place really grows on you
and now it's time to play
I'll set aside some quality time
then settle down by the TV
all of this for a cute little smile
and a mere one pound fifty!

Michael Lyons

A Feathered Thought

Have you ever thought about a swan, white as the driven snow
About her elegance of movement, quiet and gracefully slow
Her dance routine a picture as she circles round and sways
Think about a beautiful swan perfect in many ways.

Think about her nesting, peep into her mating hedge
Capture her sight of wonderful glow as she ripples the water's edge
Wingspan of softest feather guarding her offspring well
Nesting happily in the reeds, casting her swan-like spell.

Beautiful neck upright and straight, her head towards the sky
Do you think she's saying to everyone 'Look at me, I was born to fly'
Shape of her head just right, loving eyes so tenderly warm
Toning in with nature, truly a magnificent form.

How do you think a swan feels if someone raids her mothering nest
How will she suffer the agony if pellets enter he breast
How could actions be so cruel, who could wish to harm this bird
Performing diabolical torture, completely utterly absurd.

Why are some doomed to die when they get caught up in oil
Could it be they're just too beautiful, dark waters flow to spoil
Never heeding her tenderness her slinky body white and pure
Her need for full protection, or else her growing family fewer.

Think deep about a swan as she dances on her travelling lake
Teach everything in her favour, harmless give and take
So lovely is this feathered friend as her shell breaks to hatch
So perfect is this creature, no other bird can ever match . . .

Anne Kerr

I Am Just A Seal

Hit me with your club
And cave in my skull
You are much more powerful than me
And yet your intelligence is nil
For here I once did roam
I played on beautiful sea foam
My face is also beautiful
But you choose to rob me from my home
You think we aren't aware
Someone is watching from above
But you deny by killing us
The existence of God
And of nature's true love
What will you do with my body after
Sell my skin
To be made into a coat or a glove
One day you may be in my place
In a place that you once did roam
Somewhere that you once truly loved
Extinct
Without a home

Jeff D Hibbard

Secretive Cats

What is it you do,
When you stay out all night?
Where is it you go,
When the moon shines bright?
How far do you go to find your food?
If it rains out there,
Are you still in the mood?
Do you meet your friends
Round the corner, at ten?
And all sneak away
To your private den?
Where is it you sleep,
Before you come in?
Have you had a fight
... Or raided a bin?

Jennifer A Hayes

The Bleak Mid-Winter

In the morning it's still dark,
When I take Porky for his walk,
And when I get back home at night,
There is no longer any light,
But Porky cares not a jot,
As long as he gets out for his trot.

Gaily he flips his leg in the air,
As he widdles everywhere
Every blade of grass he sniffs,
He doesn't care if I'm frozen stiff,
Or if I'm wet through to the skin,
As long as he gets his walkies in.

M Brindley

WHO'S A CLEVER BOY

I am a dog
My name is Jo
Over the park is where I go.
My mistress thinks I'm very clever
For I don't mess in the garden, ever.
If I'm caught short along the road
Why I just stop and drop my load.
Wherever you go you'll find I've been
For everywhere is my latrine.
I love to beg or fetch a stick
Give a baby's face a lick.
Bark at strangers, chase a ball
Chew the door mat in the hall.
But, when nature calls me to perform
I certainly don't do it on our lawn
Oh no!
I run off quickly to the park
There in a sunlit daisy ring
I lay my steaming mark.
So when next you walk to admire the view
Spare a thought on what we doggies do.
Then I think you'll have to admit
Man's best friend is
One hell of a sh**.

S Nicolaou

The Day I Finished With My Girlfriend

It is just a young fox amongst the cats,
not a visitor this night knocking the flap.
Past Misto's and Tabs; madam and flirt
sitting nonchalant, the fox moves forward
to the food bowl, where KP Squeak sits,
nothing doing, beside it.

The fox tucks in, and the ladies powder their noses,
but the guard of the yard hears the crunching fox
and comes out sniffing.
He's a Bonnie terror, looks like a werewolf,
and he thinks he is one,
but due where it's due
he's right on cue
can't have strangers
wandering the boudoir.

The fox fled, and the cats showed a leg,
as the guardian padded indoors.
Mission accomplished . . . Sir!
Then he farts, nicks your chair
and threatens to pee
if you don't take him out, pronto,
but that's how I like my friends,
stubborn, free thinking, and furry,
and there, when I need them.

Lawrence Richards

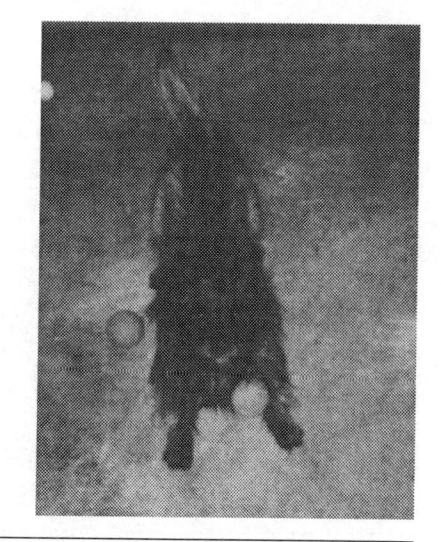

Mitzy

A little cat full of joy,
Are you a girl or boy?

Four little paws all clean and white,
Silky black fur shining bright,
I'll take you home for just one night.

You licked my hand to say hello,
I knew then, I could not let you go.

Sometimes we play, or sit in the sun
You run around, we do have fun.

You keep me happy, when I am sad
You are the best friend, I have ever had.

You will always be for me
My one and only Mitzy.

Iris Simmonds

LITTLE KOE

A mischievous little horse am I,
Pretty, well muscled, and have a kind eye,
I move with grace when I prance,
Some think I'm having a little dance.

With nimble hooves and flowing tail,
I take my rider up hill, down dale,
I spook at squirrels and race the deer,
And act as though I have no fear.

Cyclists are my latest game,
To overtake them is my aim.
On the hills they suddenly stop,
I pass and beat them to the top.

Competitions are such fun,
I prance and buck in the sun,
Then I settle and try to work,
Surprises sometimes in corners lurk.

In the field, a roll is a must,
Especially if there's plenty of dust,
Then I buck and race around,
Oh what fun to leap and bound.

In spite of this, I've a loving heart,
From my owner I don't wish to part.
On her shoulder I rest my head,
So many things yet to be said.

Janet Boulton

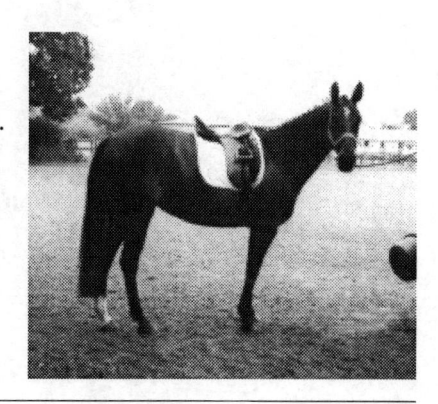

Felix

Felix didn't want much in life,
A slice of ham every now and then,
If he heard the fridge door
He'd soon be begging for more.

He would sit in the garden for hours,
Soaking up the sun and smelling the flowers.
Curled up in a little ball,
Fast asleep until he heard me call.

His *Daddy* would have a choc ice,
Felix would sit and think, 'that looks nice',
And of course he would get some,
He would lick and lick until it was all gone.

He also loved to be loved,
He didn't like to be fussed,
But the odd stroke now and then,
Was of course a must.

Helen Marie Cairns

Meg

I knew a lovely little dog,
She wasn't really mine.
But she often came to visit,
She really was divine.

She had a dark grey shaggy coat,
And eyes of liquid blue,
Which really made your heart to melt,
When they looked up at you.

When she walked in, she was in charge,
She'd lie upon the floor
Half asleep, but ears alert,
In case a knock came on the door.

Then she would soon be wide awake,
Waiting to see, who was out there,
Standing on guard, close by your side,
You felt quite safe when in her care.

Iris Covell

A Dog Called 'Suzi'

I have a border collie, and she is my best friend,
She is totally devoted, with love that knows no end.

I know of course she cannot smile, but neither does she frown,
She's never, ever cross with me, and never lets me down.

When I go out and leave her, she always looks so sad,
But when I come home she greets me, and is oh so very glad.

She looks at me with soft brown eyes, eyes that say it all,
Pleading for a tit-bit, or perhaps a game of ball.

A love like this is priceless, a love that can't be bought,
She gives her *all* completely, without a second thought.

Betty Bramma

TRAIL OF TEARS

I don't know where I have found all the tears
that I have cried for our animal friends.
Everywhere and anywhere our friends
are suffering abuse at the hands of humans.
I feel their pain so profusely that their
suffering is slowly killing me.

I feel that we should have a national crying day
where the whole world can hang their heads in shame.
There are millions of our friends suffering and dying
in laboratories and factory farms all over the world.
The only crime they are guilty of
is that of being innocent and vulnerable,
yet they often suffer incredible torture at the hands
of mankind and man is certainly not kind.

Let's hope it won't be a cold day in hell
before all men can find the compassion
in their hearts to love all God's creatures.
Amen.

Spike

From Hutch To Heaven

Listen! Listen to the munching
the munch of little jaws.
The click of teeth on water spouts,
The silent lick of paws.
Contentment nestled in the hay
to sleep or chew at will,
For a cavie's tum is never full
with hay around to fill.
These gentle little creatures
respond to love and care,
They look to us for food and warmth
for it's us that put them there!

Jean Castle

SABRE

It was a cold night, one winter
When he walked into our lives,
He looked sad and lonely
So bewildered and lost
His back was all bony
Fur hardened with frost
A big dog barely alive.

He walked into the hallway
Tail dragging behind,
Desperate to leave the streets
Searching for a home,
Longing to rest his weary feet,
He wasn't born to roam,
He was born a homely kind.

He took refuge in the yard,
Sleeping in the shed
Opposite our buildings,
He heard the human sounds inside
And though our food had filled him
Sat on the stony ground and cried,
He wanted love instead.

Stephanie Churchill

You Love Me

I am smart
like a work of art.
I play my part,
and I make you love me.

I strut my stuff
in my black coat of fluff
trimmed with a white muff,
and I make you love me.

You feed me
when I see
it's time for my tea,
and I make you love me.

I sleep all day
and all night I play
just to hear you say,
you love me.

I am your cat
and more than that
I am sat,
on your lap because you love me.

You stroke my fur
and all day I purr
I will not stop, I will not stir
because I love you.

R Medland

Flossie

My cat's inquisitive mind
so curious to the end
chased anything it could find
Flossie drives me 'round the bend'!

That nosy little feline
she made a silly bee-line
chased a great big bumble bee
where'd it go she had to see
flew into its hidey-hole
put its nose in poor wee soul
didn't know it was so young
disturb big bees you'll get stung
with her paw she poked the hive
Flossie lucky she's alive
she poked it more with her snout
the angry bees all buzzed out
Flossie felt a foolish thing
when she felt the big bee's sting
bees kept Flossie on her toes
with her swollen big red nose!

My loving cat named Flossie
that day was much too bossy
the big bees formed a posse
to sting and sort out Flossie.

My cat's inquisitive mind
is not so curious now
Flossie's sorry she did find
bumble bees can sting - and how!

Wm Chapman

Pirate Whalers

Beautiful creatures of the sea
Why should man be so greedy?
For in your flesh you retain
Monetary values for man to gain

In your thousands you are killed
For your breeding to be stilled
Barbaric rituals on the high seas
Mass slaughter of your species

Compassion and sensitivity you possess
Warm blooded mammals just like us
Highly intelligent you feel pain
Put human predator to shame

You breathe air into your lung
Bear in your womb your young
And suckle them with your milk
Sheltered by mother in an attack!

You capacitate a larger brain
Than any other creature known
You communicate over a vast range
With echoes weird and strange

You possess no natural enemies
Isn't that wonderful for your species?
But man harpoons to slaughter
First the calf then the mother

You the beast that resembles man
You could face near extinction
Death of you should be banned
Some people's pleas have been shunned

Pirate whalers ride the waves
Gunners blast with cunning ruses
Harpoons deep into the animal's flesh
Trapped by the umbrella-like mesh
The vital part in the whale's back
Is caught in the gunner's attack
Blessings should it die instantly
Sorrows should it die slowly

You the gentle giant instilling love
Grace and elegance like of the dove
Why is man so greedy?
To spread red blood into the sea.

Luciene Azique

Topsy

Topsy was an orphan mog,
Raised by humans and a dog,
Thrown out at birth and left to die,
With a tiny brother, I don't know why!

Her brother died when they'd been saved
From their dreadful plight, caused by those depraved;
But she was not about to die,
From each end of the cattery you could hear her cry.

A tiny scrap with big eyes of blue,
She knew by instinct what to do:
If her foster family would not let her feed,
Then humans must supply her need.

She never looked back once at home with me,
But wouldn't sit upon my knee.
Always active, on the go,
Any drawn up lines she refused to toe.

No written concepts apply to her,
This independent scrap of fur.
She plays for hours upon her own,
Quite different to any other cat I've known.

Sometimes aloof, people she'll ignore,
Run out when someone's at the door.
Then sometimes me with love she'll shower,
Rub, lick, knead, purr with all her power.

She stands on two legs quite easily
And can run to the top of a vertical tree.
Does she know she's a cat? Is a thought to mull,
But at least life with her is never dull!

T Betty Chadwick

Sinead Called Her Connie

She crouches on her shelf,
radiator warm, calm,
inscrutable, offered
a finger, a toy, she deigns
one soft paw, momentarily,
then withdraws into
her own world, unblinking
eyes reflecting the lights
beyond the window.
We look out, striving to see,
to experience her ways,
her thoughts: in vain.
Turning, we find her,
a ball of black fur.
She sleeps, one step ahead of us,
once again.

Robert E Fairclough

CRUEL FOOL

When nobody else wanted me,
he stood by my side.
When nobody else needed me,
he walked beside me with pride.
He loved and cared for me
like the mother I never had,
and now that he's gone
I'm feeling worse than sad.
Who could be so mean, cold hearted and cruel
half kill my friend then leave him for a fool
left him in that state,
him my only mate.
But he found his way, to my lovin' arms
and healed up so fine.
My only friend my caring friend
that faithful dog of mine.

Josephine McGaughran

The Camel And The Otter

One summer day, at half past two,
There were dark clouds above the zoo,
And though the morning had been warm,
One camel said, 'I think a storm
Is in the offing.' Said another,
'I agree. We must take cover
Right away. I'm not a one
For getting wet, I like the sun.
In fact I do prefer it hotter.'
'Don't be silly,' said an otter,
'There ain't nothing beats the water.
If you're in a zoo you oughtta
Learn to live with cold and wet
Because you're not a flaming pet.'
Said the camel, 'Do be quiet.
This is really not my climate.
Give me deserts. Give me sand.
I really cannot understand
Quite how I find myself to be
In Britain, when it's clearly plain to see
Of the desert - I'm a ship,
So don't you give me any lip
Little one. How would you feel
If your skin began to peel
From too much bathing in the sun?
I'll bet you wouldn't think it fun.'
Otter said, 'Don't think you're clever,
Coz the chance is I will never
Find me on a foreign shore.
In fact I'll be extinct before
I'm ever in a zoo abroad
Getting sunburnt, feeling bored.'
Otter, muttering, departed
As the heavy rainfall started.

James Cuin

Sheba

Once you had met her, try as you may
You would never forget her, for many a day
Sheba was regal, proud as her name
Gentle yet tough, and always the same
Loving and giving with kindness untold
Only one description - the wealth of Black Gold.

Always the mother, let him go first
He had the best bits, she had the worst
It wasn't her nature to push to the fore
She knew in her heart there would always be more
Waited patiently till she was told
I will never forget - my wealth of Black Gold.

And now she has gone, I miss her so much
Coat black and shiny, so soft to the touch
The love in her eyes as she looked up at you
Each day she would bring some pleasure anew
Love warm and tender to have and to hold
I'll always remember - her wealth of Black Gold.

Joan Walker

The Vanishing Weersigonn

The vanishing Weersigonn is extremely rare,
It has a hooked beak, a silken plumage, no hair,
Its talons are sturdy, as strong as an eagle's,
It drinks from the rivers and feeds on black beetles.

Ornithologists think it's absurd
That I have sighted this elusive bird,
I picked up my camera to take a quick snap,
It looked at me cockeyed and was gone in a flash.

It disappeared
As if by magic,
Before I could blink
The vanishing Weersigonn
Hasn't been seen since!

Glenn R Lumb

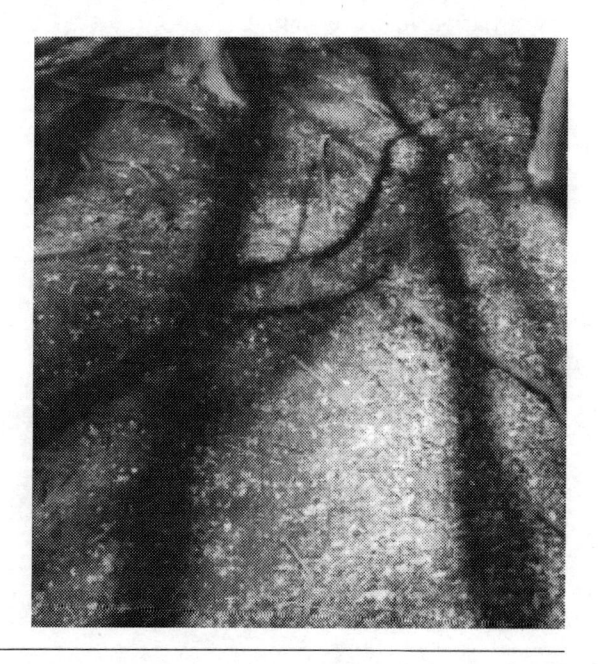

Pavy

I held her cupped in the palm of my hand,
soft, downy white kitten, struggling to stand.
I felt her small heart beat with thrusting life,
Paws, smooth as velvet, quivering to alight.

I watched her first steps, light as thistledown,
side-stepping, springing, scarce touching the ground,
leaping, dancing, joy, unbelievable,
buoyant, agile, spirit intangible.

Dainty white kitten, belovèd Pavy.
She would skip to greet us with gaiety,
springing, lithesome, alert at our calling,
proud tail raised, gleaming fur, eager purring.

To us she was the light of the morning,
new joy and delight ever unfolding,
perfect white fur of virgin purity,
her eyes, blue grey, deep pools of mystery.

One day we could not find her anywhere.
We searched and cried with growing despair.
We called her name, praying she would hear,
if, in some dark place she hid in fear.

At midnight we heard a plaintive cry.
Frantically, we traced it to a shed nearby.
We roused a neighbour, who unlocked a door.
We found her, crouched, petrified, on the floor.

Ten years we loved her for her gentleness.
We wept at the fading of her brightness.
Deep grief, with gnawing guilt at her parting,
The magic of her life, a grateful memory.

Iris Jones

I Am The Tiger

I stalk my prey then go in for the kill,
I have no friends except my brothers and sisters,
I am the most powerful, bold, and most feared.
The humans are an exception, *I* am terrified of them.
They are calculating, conspiring and hunt me for my skin,
However fast I run, however well I hide,
they're one step ahead.
Stalking me and then going in for the kill.

Hilary Beevers (13)

It's A Dog's Life

'It's a dog's life' the old saying goes,
but irony jumps out and bellows -
If only you knew what it was to be
a pig - and then you would see
that the dog's life is one to behold,
a dream - which lies dormant and cold.
It will not be because I'm a sow
and so to the dog I'm forced to bow.
Him with respect, but then that's OK,
as maybe they will like *me* one day.
Take me in, and cosset and love
seeing its worth to the good Lord above.
An animal lover, 'well, that's worth a point'
they think to themselves, as they prepare the joint
To give to the dog who gets only the best,
'It's a dog's life...'
when can I be his guest?

Alison Hawtin-Dumbrava

IN MY HEART

In the early morning light you left the door,
Through which you would return no more.
A car struck you and left you there,
You died knowing that we all care.
Tiger, I didn't have a chance to say goodbye,
But I cried for you I didn't know how you could die.
I have to come to terms with how sad I feel,
And in time I know the pain will heal.
Fifteen years of love have come to an end,
But forever we will be eternal friends.

Jo Upton

WESLEY THE WESTIE UPDATE

Wesley the Westie's now
Three years old.
He's playful, lively and
Always bold.

Still likes chewing slippers
And sweaters,
Tormenting his elders
And betters.

When the bell rings he barks
Very loud.
Of being a good watchdog
He is proud.

He guards us all fiercely
Night and day.
No-one enters without
Wesley's say.

He has a voracious
Appetite.
Wolfs his meal down so fast
Quite a sight.

But he's loving, gentle,
Faithful, true.
He stays near my side till
Day is through.

Wesley the Westie's my
Dearest friend.
On his loyalty I
Can depend.

Eileen M Ward

Waiting To Be Chosen

Sometimes I feel unhappy, it seems an age since I came here
I get so bewildered just trying to remember my past
Farmyard noises crowd my mind, why I left is not very clear.
Perhaps I was not strong enough for sheep work, became outcast.

The concrete floor and wire fronted pen really cramped my style
No way could I use up all my pent-up energy like this.
I longed for freedom to roam hedges and run mile after mile
Occasional exercise with kind ladies were times of bliss.

The staff grew fond of me I was part and parcel of the place
So I graduated to the office, enjoyed my life more.
Maybe a better chance of having a home from my new base
Now I would be the first resident to be seen by the door!

Dogs were walked by prospective owners and quite often snapped up
One day a man tried two but they didn't suit, how did they gaffe?
'What about Ajax, we've had him almost a year from a pup.'
'Oh, now he's lovely, I thought he belonged to one of the staff!'

My new owner bought me feeding bowls, toys, a collar and lead
Whilst I sat and took a last look round and hoping for a good home.
I realise I struck lucky, I can run freely with speed
Across fields or through woods then have my coat groomed
                                              with my own comb.

Mary E Beale

A Dog And His Problem

I have a staffie, as good as gold,
and he looks a real proper toff,
and so together, he and I, for the dog show, we set off.
I paid my fee, and strolled around,
till the show, it did begin.
My number called, with dog at heel, the ring I entered in.
I led him smartly round the ring, all hopes on him, I'd pinned.
But there was something not quite right,
my dog, he had, the wind . . .
the judge, a very kindly soul, said, 'Well I do declare
I'm just very thankful, this show is in the open air,
just take him for a walk,' he said,
'feel no shame, or care, bring him back in a little while,
we will move, just over there.'
We walked around, and people stared,
some did not find it funny,
'We've not come here to smell your dog, what a waste of money.'
I took him back, for another crack,
and he did not let me down,
he was the best at everything, obedience, stature, colour,
he sat . . . he stayed . . . he fetched . . . he lay,
better than any other,
the judges talked, and then did say,
'This dog again has sinned,
we really must disqualify the staffie, with the wind.'
But with the crowd behind him now, for he their hearts had won,
said they'd give him another chance.
Come on . . . come on my son . . .
through our paces, one more time,
me and my little sinner, and how proud I felt,

as I held my nose,
he was declared the winner.

Jacqueline Claire Davies

SQUIRREL (NIPPER) REMEMBERED

How you have humbled me
Bright-eyed wild creature,
Honouring me with your innocent trust.

Daily you came to me,
Tapped on my window
Asking for extras to feed to your young.

Now they too, visit me
Joyfully playing,
Recalling the days when first you appeared.

Now all that's left of you
Is that bright spirit
Sparkling like gems in the eyes of your young.

Mary Ethridge

CAGED BEAST

Hushed human voices talking
feline ears alert
soft padded paws stalking
whiskers twitching
yellow predator-eyes staring
trapped behind bars
hungry tiger-eyes glaring
black-striped cat
fur-covered shoulders power-packed
latent muscle
patrolling, pacing, movement tracked
respectful, wary
mind full of freedom dreams
jungle fever
claws and teeth, dying screams
warming rain
distant memory, shadows calling
sweltered heat
hunting, killing, paws mauling
savaged flesh
ancient cunning in every ounce
caged beast
biding time, waiting to pounce
shackled heart
spirit unbroken, yearning for home
call of the wild
untethered soul, free to roam

Paul Birkitt

Animal Love

The crofter looked out o'er windswept moor
A sound he knew well made him rush to the door
The far bleat of a lamb its cry weak and forlorn
Urged him to light lantern and strike out in the storm

His old grey mack battered and torn
Billowed and flapped in the raging storm
His eyes now stinging in the frosty air
Were blurred and half-closed as he struggled unaware

The lamb he found on a crag high in the storm
Shivering and abandoned in the breaking dawn
Care-worn hands with the tender touch caressed
the lamb that meant so much
Filled now with hope and life anew
He stumbled home with his prize warm and true.

Doris Hoole

Kitten Of My Dreams

The day I was born . . .
Was the day I met you,
You took my hand
And sang to me . . . a lullaby . . .
I would listen so carefully,
My eyes would close
And I would drift away
Into a peaceful sleep . . .
In my dreams I'd see
A little kitten appear
And run into my arms . . .
Now, a few years later,
My dream came true . . .
I had a little kitten
Of my very own . . .
He was beautiful and playful,
And he was mine!
A little later, that beautiful kitten
Grew into a beautiful cat,
And lost an eye!
But he is still the kitten of my dreams,
And I love him so.

Miran McEntee

WEE MAC

You'll always get a welcome,
   When you come in the door,
'Cos to a dog, it makes no difference,
   If you are rich, or poor.

They're not like some young children,
   Who sometimes, can be rude,
For all they want, is to go for walks,
   And get their daily food.

They sense, when you are happy,
   Or if you're feeling sad,
And when you raise your voice to them,
   They know, that they've been bad.

I tell 'Wee Mac' all my troubles,
   And I'm sure, he understands,
Because he sits, and gazes in my face,
   Slowly licking at my hands.

Jean Hendrie

My Budgies

My two budgies are my noisy friends,
It's on me they depend.
I clean and feed them every day,
They talk to me they've a lot to say.
Micky the baby he is yellow and blue,
Noddy is older, white, with a bit of blue too,
Come out of their cage and fly like mad,
If they don't come out they won't be sad.
It's getting late they won't fly in,
My, they are causing quite a din.
When they are out they peck my plants,
Love my music and want to dance.
Lots of toys and swings to play,
Whistle and play most of the day.
In summer I take their cage outside,
Watching wild birds as they glide,
I wouldn't be without my noisy birds,
Even when they get on my nerves.

Christine Kowalkowski

WARNING! BUDGIE ON THE LOOSE

Our budgie's a cute little bird
And always repeats whatever he's heard.
To the man I said, 'The rent I can't pay'
The bird will tell my husband later on today
When out of the cage he swings on the light
Then zooms round the room like a plane in flight
He aims himself at the sleeping cat's head
Lands just like a helicopter returning to base
The cat opens one eye then goes back to playing dead
The kids stay upstairs till he's back behind bars
Catching him could literally take hours and hours
He's a crafty beast lands on the table top
I think now I've got him, I pounce, then he's off like a shot
He pecks at the wallpaper leaves bare patches behind
I'm glad he's not twins I'd be out of my mind
He sits on the fish tank and annoys the fish
Think I'll get a piranha, if only, I wish
I sit to read the paper in my favourite chair
As sure as eggs is eggs he lands on my hair
I then make a grab and put him back behind bars
Round and round on his perch, he swings like a gymnastic star
I clean up the room of the budgie's devastation
A voice says 'Get in the car and go to the station'
I collect my husband at five, it's quarter to on the clock
The budgie's redeemed himself so now he can stop
But he gave me quite a shock

Irene Witte

Dolphins

Dolphins are intelligent friendly creatures,
The familiar smile is one of their features.
In the water they play,
For largest part of the day.
They have steely grey backs,
And protect their young from shark attacks.
Every two or three years they breed,
Co-operative behaviour for survival they need,
They communicate with whistles and clicks,
At zoos you see them doing tricks.
Sometimes dolphins get beached on the shore,
They have one set of teeth in a lifetime, no more.
Hunting fish when migrating in shoals,
Dolphins breathe through their blow holes.
Very friendly sensible animals,
Best known and loved of all marine mammals.

K Brown

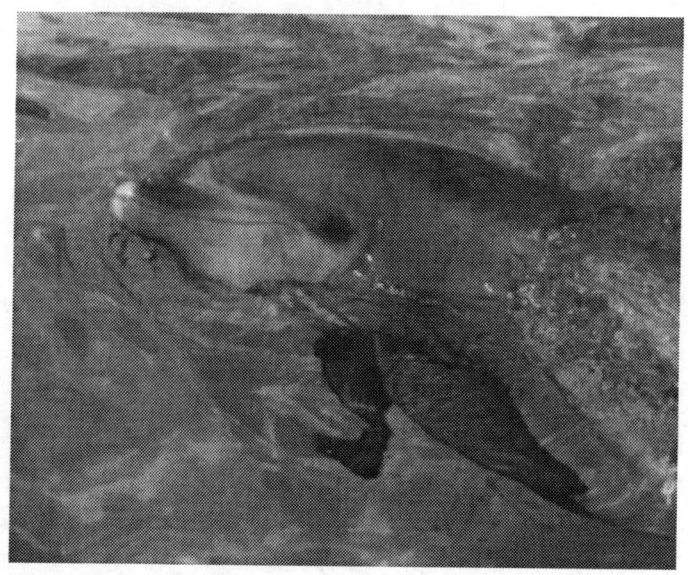

Pride Of Love

In their eyes still lives a memory
And a dream that can never die
A love engraved on a distant prayer
That we hear when their souls are nigh

While love procured their loyalty
We were beckoned by a royal command
Has soldiers of a feline sanctuary
And the defence of their sacred land

The garden was their noble territory
For the pride of love to roam
Their own African savannah
And the realm of their surrogate throne

The streets were a sabbatical adventure
Our house their religious domain
And we were the perennial servants
Put on Earth to pamper their reign

Intelligence followed with every stride
They would know when the clock had sang
With a cunning feline intuition
They would appear when the meal bell rang

They would pose as sleeping sentinels
Guarding the secret of their treasured cream
Lying in front of the colonial fire
Sometimes sharing an inaugural dream

Together was always their destiny
And eternally they shall never part
They shall prowl the streets of heaven
And the spiritual love of our hearts

David Bridgewater

Snout In The Trough

Snuffling
truffling
snout in the trough
curly corkscrew tail
twitching
pink wrinkled skin
beady eyes
snorting
cavorting
wallowing in the mud
home in the sty
grunting
hunting
in swill
dirt-splashed
full of good luck
covered in muck

Chris Bailey

Cat Moods

Out through the front door
Back through the cat-flap;
Quick rush at legs to show
Feeding bowl's empty
Or, worse, its contents
Lacks pristine freshness!
Then back in garden to
Re-mark his territory
Against invasion by
Next door marauder

Flopped out in blissful ease
Golden and white fur
Soaking the fire's heat;
Front paws crossed neatly
Till, almost too hot,
Rolls onto back with hips
Twisted to one side
Shoulders the other,
One leg stuck upwards
Like a small flagpole.

Smug in my bedroom -
After the needle-sharp
Kneading through blankets -
Presses his warm shape
Close to my body;
His rhythmic purring
More sleep inducing
Than any medicine;
Prelude to hours of peace
Till the dawn chorus.

Nancy Leeson

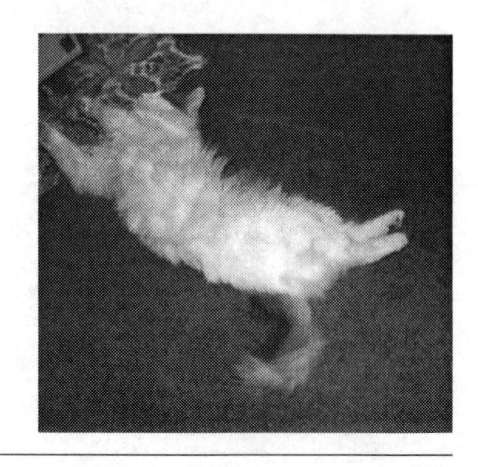

RINGO

Long spikes of hair fall over his nose
As scathing looks at me he throws.
He squeaks his orders with military flair
And at each little 'eek' he jumps in the air.

He seems sweet enough - too good to be true
But once you know him that image is through.
Nibbling fingers is his speciality
And frequently attempts to set himself free.

A natural lawnmower, he chews with speed
And his whines grow louder at his stomach's needs.
But although our disagreements are often big
He will always remain my lovable guinea pig.

Dawn-Marie Gibbons

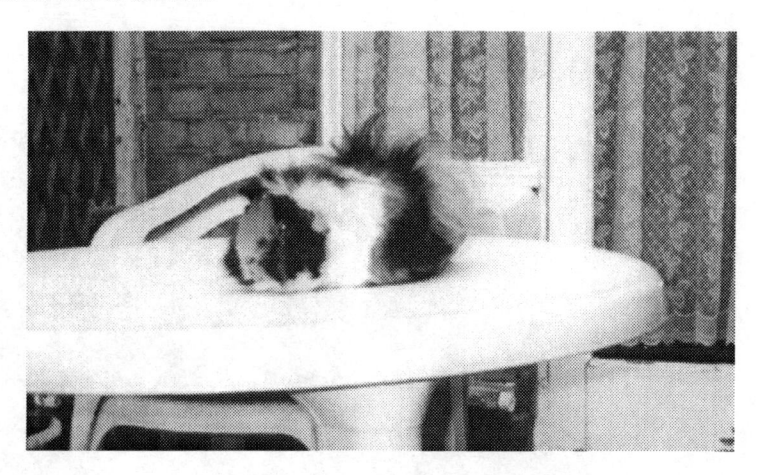

KILLER ON THE COUCH

Limbs stretched out
sleeping peacefully
ears and tail twitching
sharp teeth and claws sheathed
innocently hidden away
purring contented
whiskered head resting
upon the scattered cushions
soft features all cuddly charm
disguising your true identity
hunter's paws
stalking stealthily
fast as lightning
killing claws and toothsome jaws
death dealing feline
showing no mercy

Chris Birkitt

AMY

Sweet cat, blue cat,
Almost brand new cat,
Round cat, found cat too;
Small cat, tall cat,
Sleeping on the wall cat,
I like cats like you.

New day, every day,
Likes to dream her time away,
Never misses mealtimes once;
Fur ball, walks tall, rolls into a tiny ball,
Wriggle and run then - pounce!

Patting flowers, summer days,
Happy hours, Amy plays,
Bouncing in the sun,
One day went away,
Had to leave me, couldn't stay,
How I miss your fun.

Sweet cat, blue cat,
Too good to be true cat,
Where are you?

Alyson Mountjoy

Nikki The Mischievous Cat

Nikki is a curious cat;
Not really a friendly mate.
Sleek slender and solemn,
Who knows what might be her fate.

Twinkle in her eye,
And fortune in her gaze.
She's a loving go lucky cat,
Maybe she's going through a phase

Black as coal is her coat;
White marks the spot of her femininity,
And she doesn't know right from wrong;
Whereas her amber eyes give her anonymity.

Like a woman she has mystique,
And never shows her true feelings.
When playing imaginary hide and seek;
She usually ends up near the ceiling.

All one can do is love her;
With all her crazy faults.
Knowing our luck;
She'll end up in the vaults

Complicated is her mind;
If there is one to be found.
But to look after her
You'd be duty-bound.

Alastair Buchanan

Danny

You're an angel, an eternal flame,
burning away within my heart.
But even now that you've gone,
we're never apart.
'Cos you live on in the air that I breathe,
and everything that I see.
Still the bitter taste of death,
lies inside of me.
'Cos it took away the only friend I knew
So the evil deed was done,
but I wish it wasn't true.
Like a creature of the night,
it came then left without a trace.
Now memories are all I have,
of your sweet and lovely face.
So I wonder why mother nature,
made such a blunder.
When the pain's worse,
than rain or thunder.

Mandy Biro

Here To Stay

At time of need
You're there for me
You do not judge
Of this you're free

There is no trial
No probes to ask
Only to give
Your loyal task

When I'm alone
You will be there
To ease my fears
To rid despair

You may be old
A little slow
But you and me
Will ever grow

The tears dissolve
When you appear
To steal the pain
My mind to clear

Oh I may look
Distressed and torn
But you'll not see
My soul is worn

To give your love
Beside you lay
You're here for me
Yes, here to stay

Pauline Jones

Friendly

We had a dog called Friendly,
what a damn stupid name to call
A Jack Russell dog that was all teeth and fur,
who was not very friendly at all.
He would hide by the hedge on a summer's eve,
ready to chase and to rankle.
The women returning from the bingo hall,
whom he would immediately grab by the ankle.

He was not vindictive, of that I am sure,
his motives had nothing to do.
With the fact they were women who walked down the road,
because he would do the same thing to you.
Now Friendly would fight anything on four legs,
no matter if it were dog or a bitch.
He viewed that we all, are equal in life,
so he'd bite you if you were poor or you're rich.

Now his favourite food was chicken,
which he never refused as a rule.
If we had it for lunch his excitement was great,
and he would bounce up and down like a ball.
Now Friendly moved on to a better place,
and if there is something I am certainly sure.
He is chasing the angels around heaven above,
and nipping their ankles galore.

David Galvin

Us And Them

Us: We're off for a scenic country drive,
with maybe a stop at a pub.
If we find a good spot for a picnic,
we've brought along plenty of grub.
Have a nice chat as we go along;
catch up with the gossip and rumour.
But it all depends on those two in front,
renowned for their sense of humour.
Loopy's really a pain in the neck
and Nobby's a right little blighter.
That's why there's so many of us piled on here -
they're worse when the vehicle's lighter.
Who's got the map? Now don't lose the way!
I don't like the look of the weather.
I wonder how they'll behave today?
As usual, go hell for leather.
Still, we love them to bits, we make a good team,
we've had some great times together.

Them: Remember the time when we wouldn't stand still
when the brakes needed adjusting?
That was a laugh, they really got wild,
our behaviour was simply disgusting.
And the time we charged too fast through the ford.
They got soaked to the skin. Oh dear!
And the time he got off to go in the pub
and order a round of beer.
We took off up the road, he couldn't get on,
he was running behind for miles.
They eventually managed to drag him on board,
my word, that caused some smiles.

We're off! We'll lead them a merry dance.
What shall it be today?

We haven't decided - we won't miss a chance -
we'll think something up on the way.
Still, we love them to bits, we make a good team,
we have fun, what more need we say?

Claire Shellis

SHELLEY

He was sitting on the garden fence
One morning, last July.
I was reading a magazine
When his colour caught my eye.

He was too big to be a greenfinch,
And then I saw the sense.
I called to my spouse and told him,
'There's a budgie on our fence.'

My husband went out warily,
Caught the budgie in his hat.
We watched it fly around inside
Then on a plant it sat.

I asked around the neighbourhood,
I was bound to spread the word.
But no-one seemed to want to know
About this poor little bird.

Now he lives in a gilded cage
With his ladder and his toys.
He's a happy little budgerigar;
I love to hear his noise.

We have a Labrador named Byron
So we called this pet, Shelley.
We live in poetic harmony
Watching wildlife on the telly.

Sara Newby

No Other

Glossy coat, big, and bouncy,
He bounds up to greet you,
Face lit up with a smile,
Suddenly blocks your view.

After gaining your balance,
And wiping the mud off your skirt,
You say 'good boy' and stroke him,
Wondering where he got all the dirt.

He wags his tail quite furiously,
You try to get out of his way,
Being so big, his tail will thump,
And you will feel it the rest of the day.

Soft and gentle and loving is he,
In me he puts all his trust,
Very rare do I have to scald him,
Only when I know I really must.

He is a black flat-coated retriever,
And Cajun is his name,
I could never love another,
There will never be one the same.

Glennis Horne

Tadsor Arabian Stud

It's peaceful here, beneath the trees
Where the grass is ruffled by the breeze
Where brood mares graze in the morning sun
As around the fields the youngsters run.

The stables are clean and bedded with straw
The summer has dried the rain once more
Over each stable door appears
A head each wise beyond its years.

As another blissful morning dawns
In his box the stallion yawns
Here he was born and here he will stay
An idyllic existence in every way.

Margaret Lord

Kelly

She is old now
but full of love,
she gazes with seeing eyes
into my soul
somehow this gesture
makes me whole
signifies a bright new day
because the essence
is here to stay.
How fast the years have flown,
as a tiny pup
she summed me up
'yes I will do'.
The wagging tail
now old and frail
told me all I knew,
and if I forget
to comfort her
her eyes will shine
with understanding
at my neglect
and at the end of day
she still holds sway
the rightful owner
of my heart today.

Joan Hands

CHICKO

Long years ago Dad went to sea and brought a monkey home.
Dear Mother said, 'It can't stay here. Find it another home!'
But we three kids quite loved it and begged that it should stay
Assuring her we'd train it and she'd never rue the day.

Dad said 'Her name is Chicko. It's a name she seems to know.'
And the little monkey chattered as she darted to and fro.
A narrow lead restrained her which was fastened round her waist.
''twas as well we could control her as she moved around in haste.

Dad built a heated outside pen all cosy, snug and warm.
Our 'Chicko' played there happily quite safe and free from harm.
She'd sit upon a shoulder when we took her for a walk
And join in with her chatter if friends stopped to have a talk.

But several times she broke out free. The monkey then would roam
Into other people's gardens not very far from home.
She tore the flowers and blossoms from the plot across the way
And did no end of damage one lovely summer day.

An angry neighbour in distress came to us to complain.
Poor 'Chicko' caused such problems that she could no more remain
A family pet. Reluctantly, we gave her to a zoo
Where other monkeys played with her and she was happy too!

Vivienne Joyce

A Hymn For Creatures Great And Small

Dear Lord, accept the prayers we offer
For all Thy creatures in our care.
That none may suffer fear or violence,
Your guiding hand be always there.

For each and every humble sparrow,
Our Master marks their single fall.
Teach us to strive, and never weaken
The tireless fight to save them all.

Give us a heart of tender mercy,
Let no wild beast in suffering lie.
For them eternal freedom granted,
By hunter's gun no more shall die.

Far round the world this prayer is offered
For strength and guidance from above,
Make us aware of all their suffering,
And keep them in Your wondrous love.

Linda J Bodicoat

A Tree Full Of Birds

Great, Great Granddad was a carnivore,
He caught his own food, he lived in the wild.
I've been fed on mincemeat all my life,
I eat off a plate like a human child.

A tree full of birds sing so sweetly to me,
I can hear it from the end of the street.
A tree full of birds makes me feel so good,
Like a human with a bag full of sweets.

Could I leave them for you with their feathers all chewed,
Could I leave them down there on the mat?
Would you like to make them into a pie?
They're a present from Mr Cat.

I can't understand why you locked me in a room
And I can't get into the street.
I don't understand why you don't like blackbird pie
Because blackbirds are lovely to eat.

That tree full of birds sing so sweetly to me,
I can hear it out there in the street.
I don't understand why you think that it's wrong,
You'd do the same thing with a bag full of sweets.

Malcolm Lisle

Sanctuary At 'Freshfields'

High in the bleak and beautiful hills,
Surrounded by the limestone grey walls,
There lies a place of shelter and repose,
A sanctuary maintained with loving care,
A welcoming home for donkeys old and young,
Sick or neglected, forlorn or rejected,
Rejuvenated now in friendship and love.

In kind weather the green fields are their domain,
In less clement times in the barn they reside,
Their names on the stalls for all to see.
With stamping feet and ears pricked high,
Their braying voices fill the sky.
They munch their treats in noisy bliss
And what a happy sight is this?

A Holly Welcome along the walls,
A Christmas tree with coloured lights,
Four hopeful donkeys to each stall
With a stocking for gifts pinned to the door,
Seats and tables in readiness
For the carol service to be held that night.
The air of expectancy was felt by all.
There was magic in the barn that day,
In the true meaning of Christmas.

Mary Marriott

Lop Ears

'Lop ears, lop ears, to where are you bound?'
'I'm going outside to dig up the ground.
I'd rather dig carpets, but I'm not allowed.
So I go to the garden with head bowed.
I get my own back when I go inside,
I create havoc, then run and hide!
But all is well when the evenings come
I can lie by the fire, warming my tum!'

Margaret Brazier

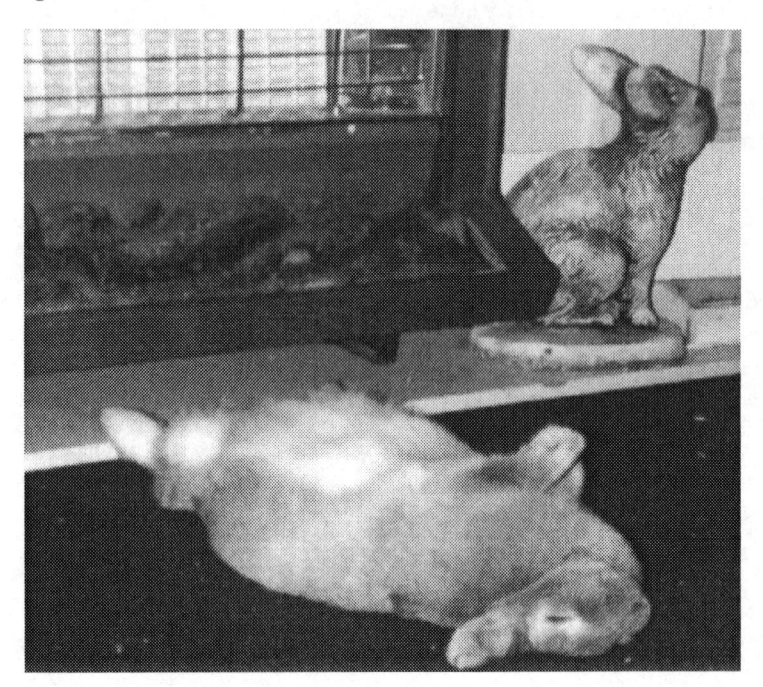

The Heart-Broken Chicken

'Oh, woe is me'
The chicken cried,
'My love has gone
To be quick fried,
That wicked farmer
Came to see
What tasty treat
He'd have for tea,
And oh, my dear
Was plucked for sure
My heart is broken
For evermore!'

Karen Jones

Old Jenny

What will you do when we're not around,
No tasty scraps upon the ground,
When the little tin huts have all gone home,
And you're left in the forest all alone.
You've always managed without our aid,
You'll have more area in which to graze.
But who will shelter you when the north winds blow,
And the grass is covered by winter snow.
Will anybody really care
That you are trying to feed where the grass is bare.
I will think of you, my little grey friend,
When north winds blow and the great oak bends.
You and your friends have given us so much pleasure
Thoughts of you we will always treasure.
And come next spring we'll be back again,
Come frost or snow, wind or rain
Your foal to see, be it jack of jenny,
And watch the wildlife, there are so many.
So enjoy your rest from us mere grockles
Who leave the litter and broken bottles.
I'll think of you when I am sad
But thoughts of you will make me glad.

Marlene S Browne

Educated Dog

I can wag my tail
and beg with my paw,
and put muddy footprints
over the floor.

I can sit when I'm told
but just for a while,
my skittish antics
make you smile.

I love to run
and jump and slide,
and sniff and explore things
far and wide.

But try as I might,
it's such a caper,
I haven't yet learned
to read the paper.

Sally Quinn

To A Cat

With black and white face a picture
and beauty most serene,
you purr when wanting petted
but snarl if not so keen.
When good looks were handed out
you were at the head of the queue.
But we know it's only skin deep,
for no-one's vicious like you.

We see you running at mealtimes,
when I whistle, you know it's out.
A whistle again at bedtime
again you're there with no doubt.
You stole the dog's bone, remember,
a bone so much bigger than you,
you growled as we approached,
the next time we bought two.

You walk down the road as you own it
cars stop to let you pass by.
Ignore them as if they're not there
with your nose and tail to the sky.
I come home from work to park up
and as I select reverse gear,
you're climbing in through the window,
with a welcome no-one should fear.

I've seen you clear a garden fence,
with one leap, onto a six feet gate.
So why when it's time for dinner
this pratt lifts you up to your plate.
Yes, Toby, it is obvious that
vicious is your middle name
and although we miss that bundle of fluff
we're ever so glad you came.

I McKenzie-Young

Triple Joy

Wiry and active
Are my dachsies three,
Violet, Minkie,
And tubby Amie.

Sleek supple bodies
And velvet brown eyes,
Three bundles of love,
So trusting and wise.

Dearest companions,
Intelligent; bright.
Out chasing rabbits -
A wonderful sight.

Short muscular legs -
Powerhouses of speed,
All thoroughly gutsy
And inclined to greed.

Dashing; delightful;
Roguish, but kind.
An unpleasant thought
Never enters their minds.

Constantly loyal -
Quick to obey,
Three very dear pals
Who brighten each day.

Betty Robertson

Suzie And Cracker

Our Suzie went 'a-courting'
Whilst on holiday in our van.
She met the cutest Yorkie,
A real young 'matcho' man.
She'll be quite safe we told ourselves,
Now she is seven years old.
But nine weeks later fate decreed
This story should be told.
One early morning, to our joy,
A pup was born;
A handsome boy!

Now Suzie and Cracker are such good friends,
A mother's patience knows no end.
She cleans and grooms him every day
He's made her young again, with play.
She's taught him how to fetch a ball,
To come at once to master's call.
To guard the house, this duty shared,
And the best place to sleep is the velvet chair!
But after a long walk and run,
It's nice to cuddle up with mum!

Cynthia Shum

Sadie

Oh weep for poor Sadie! It was a sad day
When they cut off her tail and threw it away!

When Sadie was born she was quite complete
With a head and a tail and four nice feet,
But fashion decreed that her round little rump
Would look so much better with just a short stump,

So they cut off her tail and threw it away,
Oh pity poor Sadie, oh rue the day!

Tails are for steering, for greeting, for pride,
Tails are for speaking when words are denied,
But when she is longing her love to affirm,
All Sadie can do is wriggle and squirm.

Oh weep for poor Sadie, weep for the day
When they cut off her tail and threw it away.

Fiona Ballantine

MY FRIEND

She stands tall and powerful,
Against the setting sun,
Yes, this is the beautiful horse,
That shares in all my fun.

Her black mane glistens and her eyes shine,
As she gallops on the beach.
There's something special all around us,
That only my horse and I can reach.

Her hooves send up a flying spray,
From the salty sea,
Yes, this is my Arab horse,
My best friend ever to be.

Rachel Hudson (14)

Our Pets

We had a small tabby cat,
which would sleep on the mat,
and a dog with a waggly tail,
goldfish that would swim round,
in a pond in the ground,
and terrapins that were rather frail.

We had tortoises so slow,
they did not seem to grow,
and a hare that grew ever so big,
we had rabbits for sure,
that increased by the score,
next came Donald our cute little pig.

But the best pet of all,
as I now can recall,
was a beautiful friendly crow,
he'd fly down onto our shoulder,
there was none more bolder,
as he loudly caw cawed his hello.

Pamela Eckhardt

On Walking The Dog

'Walkies!'
Spaniel, 'Silke', pricks her ears,
Leaps for lead chain,
Hauls her master
Into parkland, where
Afternoon routine begins.

Trotting smartly, tail a-wag,
She quarters the ground;
Nosing the turf,
Savouring a varied menu
Of delicious smells.

Graceful, as a ballet dancer,
She runs fast and free.
Pin-prick in foot, startles;
She leaps sideways, squealing,
As though stung by hornet!

Vanished? Lost dog!
Ah, there she is, deep
In undergrowth.
Emerges, and sits frog-like,
Shaking her long shawl-like ears
Black dusters in the wind!

Now, there's a friend,
'Jack' Russell, patch-eye.
Raucous greeting, lolling tongue.
Circling, harassing, sniffing:
'Come on. Play with me Jack!'
Boundless energy; barking
'This is fun!'

Bryan Holden

A Friend For Life

I said I wouldn't have another dog
Then you were brought to me,
You were unloved and undernourished
And as scared as you could be.

I picked you up and cuddled you,
You timidly licked my hand,
And I knew I had to keep you
Though it wasn't what I'd planned.

When my children came to visit
They laughed and said 'What's that?
Don't tell us you call that a dog,
She's just a skinny rat!'

I fed you well and loved you,
I bought you toys to play.
You soon began to fill out
And grew more confident each day.

You love having lots of visitors,
Playing with my grandchildren is great.
But you still won't let the postman in,
He leaves the letters at the gate!

You've learnt a lot of new tricks,
I laugh at your funny ways,
We've been so good for each other
You brighten up my days.

I've had you now for four months,
And I know we'll never part.
You found a home for life, Floss,
The day you touched my heart.

June Stokes

The Barn Owl

The barn owl flies on silent wings
Across the fields by night
Her ghostly form a silhouette
Against the darkened sky
She turns her head to listen
To the sounds all around
Then hovers for a second
Before swooping down
The vole below hears nothing
As he eats a juicy worm
Until a silent claw
Plucks him from the ground.

Val Reed

Don't Panic . . .?

We've had a lovely holiday in Cornwall, by the sea,
But now we're all packed up to leave - the cases, bags and me.
Mum told me, 'Sit and guard these things whilst we sweep
up your hairs,'
And dad called out how good I was, as he moved beds and chairs !
I feel so proud just sitting here, carrying out my task -
Well, what a time I've had, I mean it isn't much to ask.

It looks as though they've finished now, the chalet looks like new;
It really was a home from home for this last week or two -
I've just one thing to say now as the car is loaded up -
'For goodness sake, dear mum and dad, please don't forget your pup!'

Jenny Prescott

Ants

I'm looking at the ant
So tiny you just can see
On his own insignificant as can be
When you put a few together
How strong they can be
They can move mounds
To feed and protect their family.
This shows the wisdom of God's creation
We all stick together we can be a great nation
Man with one mind to live life for the whole.
Live as one unit in body and soul
Let all the differences be set aside, and
like the ants all think to unite, and
make our mark on this world no
matter how small.
Together we make a difference
Divided we fall
So be like the ants together unite
Make your life by example
Have stature and might.

Faith can work miracles.

Jessie Knox

WATER QUEEN IN MY HOUSE

You thrive in water,
Feed, breed and seed in water.
Swim swiftly, escape enemy also in water,
Your beautiful behaviour
With calm, cool, quite and quirk scenario
When I took you in my custody,
I feel pleasure in diverse dissipation.
In a small space you show all you possess
Compelling me to possess and confess;
Adequate -
Safety, shelter, feed, facilities, warmth wisely,
Prevention from dirt, disease, disaster, death
You live in a little glass chamber
The truth of life to be remembered
Water world in my house
Moving fast with your spouse
With all bliss of nature's pride
Seeing sea of full stride.

Amita Saxena

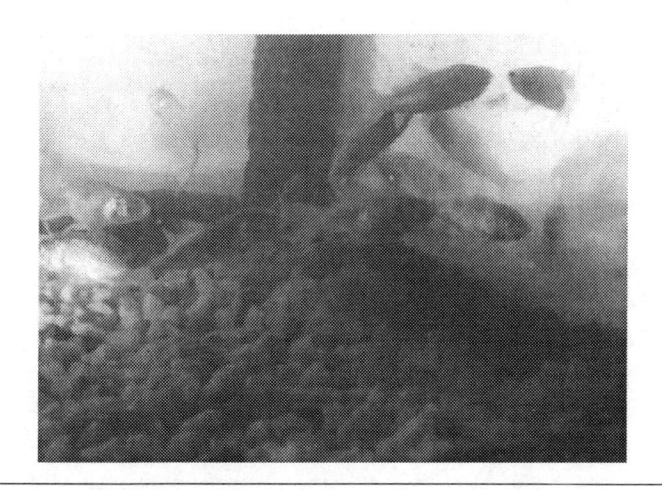

The Family Feline

Pushing through the door ajar,
He ventures to the warmth.
Surveying for a comfy lap,
On which, his fuss to flaunt.
His cheeks, he rubs, on vacant hands,
To prompt their exercise,
As sharp, his daggers penetrate,
Whilst rearranging thighs.

Sounds within the kitchen,
Will guarantee his move,
Racing to his checking point,
In hope to find fresh food.
If this you'll not endeavour,
And repeat the recent flavour,
Dissatisfied, he turns his back,
Showing instant lack of favour.

Recognising problems,
Be it illness or dismay,
Faithfully, he's at your side,
Giving comfort, night and day.
When absent, for return, he'll watch,
From windowledge, most snug,
Then greets with loving expressions,
As round your calves, he rubs.

Silken grey, his soft fur coat,
Long whiskers, slender white,
Once a hearty fighter,
Until the decline of his sight.
Still young, his personality,
Most versatile, in game,

The feline of the family;
Gaskett, is his name.

Sara Russell

TARA

My beloved pet
My greatest companion
She's so loving
Gentle and kind.

A gift to me
And to mankind
She trusts everyone
Who comes to see us.

She's a blessing
From above
She's my ears
And my guard
And she's *my love*

I know she loves us
Because she's there
At every sound
She sits and stares
Her loving brown
Eyes tell us
Someone's there

Tara my Tara
She's our best friend
She will be here
Till the end
Yes my Tara
My greatest friend.

Ruth Edna Bailey

My Dog Chips

A cuddly ball of brown and white,
Looking at you with eyes so bright
Ever faithful, loyal, loving,
And is always very trusting.

Always there whenever you call,
Ever ready to chase his ball,
Or a stick, if you are on the beach,
Even if it's beyond his reach.

When you are sad or feeling blue,
He's always there to comfort you.
When you are happy and all's well,
It's almost as if he can tell.

Of other dogs he has no fear,
Be they small or large as a deer,
He'll stand up to defend his plot,
He'll just stand firm and bark a lot.

Of children he is very fond,
Seems to have formed a husky bond,
With children living all about
Who are in our house - in and out.

Of my family he's a part,
And I love him with all my heart,
My little dog, Chips is his name,
What was it like before he came.

Rosa Butterworth

ODE TO SALLY

The hunter bounds forward,
small, red-brown and slim,
Velvet eyes sparkling,
coat smooth and trim.

With short powerful legs
and muscular paws,
She speeds over furrows,
whose dark earth she claws.

The rabbits will scatter
as forward she goes,
Racing for safety
from her long pointed nose.

Earth flying fast,
the hole she soon widens,
Only pausing to yap
at the bunny who's hiding.

Through an underground maze
her quarry escapes.
Scampering quietly,
a new route he takes.

This dachshund, now weary,
heads homeward to see
If she has been missed -
have they saved her some tea?

When well fed and tired
she creeps to her bed,
Her eyes flutter sleepily -
one thought fills her head.

There is always tomorrow,
and then - just maybe,
She'll return home triumphant -
with rabbit to eat.

Betty Robertson

BABE, MY BUDGIE

He talks to his mate from dawn till it's late
but his mate never answers him back
she's a plastic bird by the name of Kate
and she often ends up with a whack.

He gets het-up when he asks for a kiss
for Kate just sits there and looks blank
poor Babe, that's his name, would be in bliss
if Kate only showed some kind of thanks.

He waits in the morning for me to come in
with my biscuits and tea by his cage
but he wants all my biscuits and cries 'It's a sin'
then he struts up and down in a rage.

Now when he calms down he says 'Who's a good boy?'
Then he comes out and sits on my finger
he gives me a peck and I give him a toy
then it's back in the cage 'cause it's best not to linger.

Marjorie Horgan

The Hedgehog

Hedgehogs are such friendly chaps
though sleeping in the day.
Hiding in the undergrowth
or in the stacks of hay.

Prickly balls of needles, sharp
curled up there on the ground.
A guard against attackers
as they are homeward bound.

Two small eyes and ears there
amongst the spiny coat.
Beyond its mouth extending
a snout, quite long, please note.

Hunting in the darkened hours
for beetles, worms and slugs.
Helping gardeners with these pests
by eating all those bugs.

In the dusk you may just see
a hedgehog rushing by
quickly passing in a flash
on legs that simply fly.

Margaret Jackson

Animal Crazy?

Animals...
Don't get drunk
Don't get stoned
Don't waste their lives
Sitting at home.

Animals rarely kill their own race
Animals don't care
About their face.

Animals put up with a hell of a lot
From us.
The *superior* species.
But I don't think that I could thrive
Out there,
Out there
In the cold
And rain

So don't treat animals
Like they're nothing
Don't waste their lives
Cooped up at home

Don't confine them,
Torture them,
Kill them,
For our vanity.

Because animals don't mess our lives up
So don't bother destroying theirs.

Jo Sutherland

To Samson (1992-1996)

Crisp night - stars twinkling like fairy lights in the sky,
just like your eyes dear Sam,
I pray God will protect you my beloved.

Cool morning - you're dead I am told - why you?
They have killed my dear Sam,
They have murdered my beloved.

That road, those cars, I curse them all,
for the pain they have caused my dear Sam,
the suffering they have sent my beloved.

They knocked down my fairy king, they didn't care that,
broken they left my dear Sam,
dying they left my beloved.

My affectionate kitten, my sweet little friend
oh those beautiful shining eyes my dear Sam,
that were you - indeed your very soul, my beloved.

Warm evening - nightmares - he's dead I am told - why you?
They killed my dear Sam,
God did not protect my beloved.

Crisp night - start twinkling like fairy lights in the sky,
Just like how your eyes were my dear Sam,
Just as they are still - in my heart, my beloved.

Olivia Kennedy

Poppy Day

Poppy tall,
Poppy red,
Jake, my lifelong friend, is dead.

Poppy tall,
Poppy red,
It's cruel to keep him alive, they said.

Poppy wilt,
Poppy die,
It just takes a dog to make a grown man cry.

Poppy wilt,
Poppy die,
His memory lives in my tear-filled eyes.

Poppy take seed,
Poppy grow,
There's another Jake out there, that much I know.

Poppy tall,
Poppy red,
Jake, my heart and soul, is dead.

Bob Darvell

If I Were

If I were an eagle,
I would be so free,
to fly above the mountains,
over field brook and valley.

If I were a horse,
dancing in moonlight,
how I would gallop across the plains,
for my freedom I would fight.

If I were a she-wolf,
and in a forest lived,
I would hunt in the darkness,
freedom would be my gift.

If I were a dolphin,
the ocean I would swim,
living in the open sea,
far from human din,

If I were a lion,
in the jungle I would roam,
across the wilderness of Africa,
finding freedom and my home.

But alas I am a human,
and in society I must dwell,
though I long to be alone,
my freedom I must quell.

E Sturdy

Longing

I have a bird which never sings,
A bird with folded, flightless wings.
It never sits on treetops high
Nor swoops nor soars in cloudless sky.

It cannot peck the golden grain,
It cannot feel the gentle rain.
With muted voice and beak of clay,
It cannot greet the new-born day.

Fashioned by a loving hand
In a far-off foreign land,
Its head is hollow, beak shut tight,
Earthbound, silent, day and night.

From my wooden window-ledge
My bird stares out at tree and hedge.
This sad and lifeless lump of clay
Fills me with pity every day.

I see its dead and doleful eye
Staring at sparrows flitting by
And seeming to taunt my bird of clay,
Fettered forever and a day.

My bird and I, together apart,
Each with an empty, grieving heart,
Pinioned, imprisoned, we sing no song
Far, far from the land where we belong.

Megan Hughes

Brock's A 'Second'?

They told me Brock's a 'second' -
It was what they really reckoned.
No Papillon should have that broad white
      jagged band along his head.
He looked just like a badger, or so they said.
The left ear's frosted and left eye's black,
And only half a white nose band, alas, alack.

But he has grown a magnificently flowing black/white ruff
And looks just like a dancing powder puff.
His furry ears are huge and radar-tuned to any
      sound that can be heard.
He picks up every single word,
And he sports a snowy, flowing fountain of a tail.

So I've no cause to rant and rail.
As far as I am much concerned
My ugly duckling into a handsome prince
      has turned.

Eileen M Lodge

Ballad To A Pig

From coiled pert tail
To whiskered cheek,
Your soft peach skin is stretched
In glabrous sheets of unbroken line,
Reaching down to those trotting feet.

You omnivorous hoofed member of the
Suidae tribe; not known for cleansing habits,
Yet as you wallow in the mud -
Unrestricted in sensuality -
I savour your unchecked spirit

As I watch you feed your young
Awashed in milk in plenty
I catch your complacent
Gratified grunt and for seconds share
Such solemnity.

Through forest deep in fern and mulch
You snout those truffles deep.
Laboriously moving past twisted root
On old oak stump - weaving
In and out.

I sing this song to all your clan
To praise you all in abundance
These notes sail high on shifting
Breeze, capturing memorable moments,
'Pig, you glorious inhabitant.'

Joan Richardson

Tessa

You were one of our pets in a very long line,
And all of them special and really so fine.
A striking white bundle of cotton wool fur,
In a bed with your brothers not a hint of a stir.
You grew at a rate we couldn't believe.
First by my ankle then up to my knee.
You were getting so lovely a beautiful sight,
A long silky coat of a pure, pure, white.
Then it was time for a trial in a show,
We'll get you ready and away we will go.
The judge looks at you and asks you to run,
Off you go like the shot of a gun.
It was the 1st prize of many, how proud we all felt,
The look in your eyes made all the hearts melt.
'Tessa' we called you our greatest princess.

And you never seemed to get into a mess.
Show after show you just went on and on.
Rosettes and trophies, you never went wrong.
But not just the winning, you were 'Our Girl',
Many others came but you were the pearl.
We loved them all, but it was the serene face,
With dark brown eyes flanked with lashes like lace.
Your day of glory is over, but you're still our pet.
The best gentle giant we could have and ever get.
May the time pass still slowly and give us, more years,
Until we have to part and it all ends in tears.

Frances Cook

Those Mucky Geese
(Dedicated to Henry and Gemima who decided to spend the cold, icy nights of winter on our terrace rather than sleep in the barn.)

Oh, you are a mucky pair, my terrace - a disgrace
Green, sticky piles you leave there for visitors to face

Although I love you dearly, your welfare - my concern
I did not want you really, so closely to sojourn

When I survey the morning enthroned here - in my bed
I welcome noisy greeting as you wait to be fed

With joy I hear you tapping, such pleasure - you inspire
As you knock out your greeting of which you seldom tire

White necks so gently swaying, soft feathers - stirred by breeze
Impatient eyes are watching as I just take my ease

You have a barn as harbour, a shelter - from the cold
Yet you prefer your ardour the night air to enfold

When temperature is freezing and snow falls - thick and fast
You stand on terrace, wheezing, whilst moisture trickles past

Bright beak in feathers buried, eye blinking - vigil keep
Ensure my home well guarded whilst I in safety sleep

Dear mucky pair, come Springtime, sap rising - thoughts of nest
Green fields beckon, sweet, sublime. Please give my broom a rest.

Marilyn K Hambly

ALICE

A little dog - a miniature, the smallest of her class
of poodles, she would almost fit inside a lager glass
Compared to her the Yorkshire terrier seems immense
Who trots along to visit - underneath the garden fence

She's quite content - her little basket snug beside the hearth,
Her shrill bark which announces strangers on the path
Outside the door, - whilst on the floor
She leaves her favourite ball, to play with
When she hears her master's footsteps in the hall

Such tiny mites affectionate - serve many a human creed
To banish loneliness and pain, or meet a spinster's need.
Someone to love and cherish when the world has passed them by
Leaving them sad, so bad in fact that they no longer try

Those little bright eyes that respond
To each affection shown
Unwinding you, reminding you, that you are not alone
Who shares with you, and cares with you, to make your life complete
When strangers stop, outside the shop, to murmur 'Oh! How sweet!'

L T Coleman

Instincts

Dropped off on the doorstep,
The door closes and the night awaits,
He sits high and proud
The tiger of the night.
On top of the garden gate,
Stalking through the long grass
He sights his nightly prey,
Who in panic, scatter through the
Brambles, trying to get away.
But there is no escape,
He knows where they hide
And on his belly he crawls so sly,
With a deadly pounce, his jaws crush
And a small life ebbs away.
Satisfied at his kill, he leaves it for
The morn, then when his master goes to work,
He will find it neatly placed upon the lawn.

Michael Avery

To Joker

When first I saw you, you were gaunt and thin,
Your deep brown eyes were sunk and wild with fear.
To keep you so was deepest shame and sin.
I paid the price - it cost me dear,
And took you home and nursed you back to health.
You put on weight with barley hay and corn.
Your lustrous eyes and coat give me more wealth
Than I've had in the bank since I was born.
With pride you carry me through sun and rain,
Unfalteringly you leap the five-barred gate
With gaily carried tail and streaming mane.
I bless the day that sealed our fate
When loud I whistle from beside the wall
And across the meadow comes your answering call.

C L Pearson

ANIMAL CRUELTY

Animals kept away in the darkness
Sheltered from freedom and love
Neglected and put to the side to die
In pain and all alone
Animals staring with pitiful faces
At passing people with hope
Eyes full of sadness, searching for reasons
Wishing so much to belong
Animals born into this world
Powerless to cruelty
Tested on, starved, rejected,
Only ever wanting to feel love.

Beverley Wilson

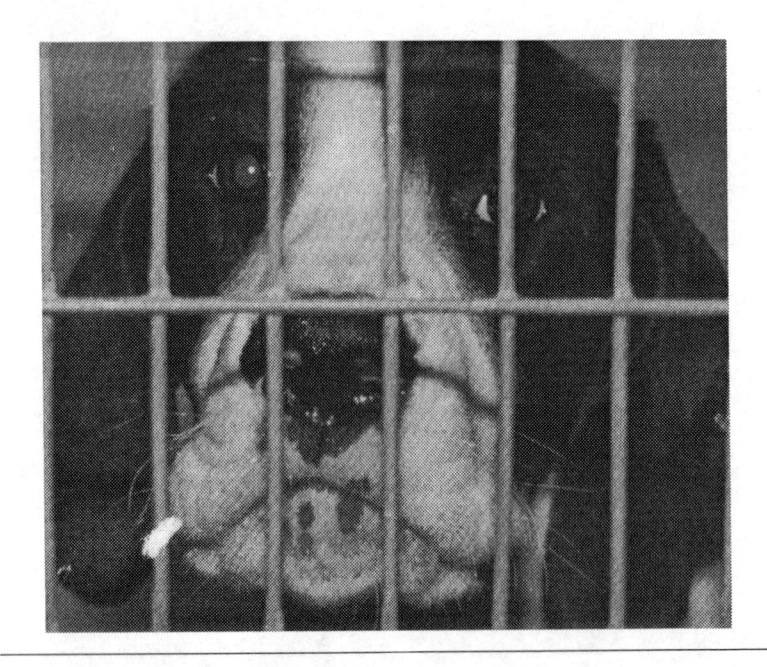

My Special Friend

She sits there so solemn,
Just watching me play.
Sitting, looking after me,
Through night and day.

She's been my lifelong friend,
All through her life and mine.
And I know some day it will happen,
Those death bells will chime.

Why did it have to happen,
That time on Christmas Day.
When she left us all,
This I have to say.

She was my special friend,
Since I was two or three.
And I knew right from the start,
That she would always be in my heart.

Emma Gale

A Visit With Libby

Libby knew she was going on a visit one summer's day
She always seemed to look forward to, in her special way
I couldn't get her choker and lead on quick enough
When she forgot her good manners, I had to be firm and a little tough

She knew where she was going, as excitement crept on
Rather she took me, instead of talking her, as she pulled along,
When at last we arrived after a long walk, mum welcomed us there
Stroking Libby's fur, which was smooth and golden fair,

With her head on one side, her paws held aloft, her tail wagging
Looking up as if to say, 'Can I come indoors, as my mistress is
                                    behind and dawdling'
Her hazel eyes looked up and down, as she asked in her way for tea
This was her favourite drink she loved, as she looked on with glee.

She would run and rush to the bowl in a jiffy
With a few gulps, she swallowed it down so quickly
She then would flop down by a chair, so careless and slack
At last when relaxing, I would put my feet on her back,

After a while, we would play games with a ball.
Catching and keeping it, until she let it fall,
Oh, what a teaser our Labrador was, but all very worthwhile,
Loved by all with her gentle ways, and her comical style,

Just after her dinner, she must have forgot she had eaten it,
Her head propped sideways, she then in her way asked for a biscuit,
But then, why not spoil animals, that we have loved and cared for
Who have brought happiness to our lives and simply had to adore,

Who meets us, and greets us, and who has visited those in the past
Never to forget those precious animals, we have sadly lost,

And never to neglect any animal, even if we are ourselves in need
If they are trained properly, you will find a faithful friend indeed.

Jean McGovern

Lucky

Ah could you tell your story,
My little purring friend
Of how much you have suffered,
As your life we try to mend;
Would you tell of life among the alleys
Or dark, cold back-street nights,
Of finding scraps in rubbish bags
Or hard won gruelling fights;
You clean yourself religiously,
Rest among my cushions with a sigh,
But sometimes I detect a glint
Of wanderlust in your eye.
You've borrowed us to suit your needs,
For you, we'll never own,
Resting in ambient solitude
Like a lord upon a throne,
You look upon us with contempt
For treating you so kind,
You came from a world so different,
Where survival of the strongest you would find;
Perhaps as you grow older
You may mellow from this way,
To be a part of our home
If you decide to stay;
So we will call you *Lucky*
Because; we think we are just that,
To have you stay at this house
Now controlled by one small *cat*.

David A Garrett

My Special Friend

My dog, my special friend
Not just a pet,
But part of me,
I'll not forget,
The pleasure that she gave.

The walks, the tempting scents,
She always made me wait.
Although I didn't mind,
I'd watch her from the gate,
She never really meant to misbehave.

And now she's gone,
My heart is full of pain,
It's anything I would do,
To have her back again,
I'm sure she knew how dear she was to me.

Now days are empty,
As I walk alone,
Along the leafy lanes,
The haunts where we would roam,
Memories remind me of her constantly.

My dog, my special friend,
Much love she had to give,
I'm sure that she would understand,
How hard I prayed for her to live,
And how things used to be.

J W Whitehead

My Brave Wally

I first saw him in a pet shop,
1987 was the year,
Other budgerigars were attacking him,
He trembled with such fear,

My heart went out I chose him,
So vulnerable and bullied,
Then clutching my six-inch box,
From the shop I hurried,

In the first few weeks it seemed,
That surely he would die,
As he kept falling from his perch,
Also he could not fly,

He would fall upon his back,
To his feet he would try to stand,
Yet always he would need me,
To give a helping hand,

Determination courage,
Has this plucky bird of mine,
With crippled feet he has battled,
And now gets along just fine,

I tickle his tum and stroke his beak,
He kisses my nose in return,
We both have trust in each other,
With a love we both had to learn,

Adorable Wally yellow and green,
Now approaching ten years of age,
The prettiest budgie in all the world,
Lives in my house in his cage.

Ann G Wallace

WHERE?

Where have all the meadows gone?
Said the rabbit to the hare,
They're buried beneath the tarmac
That 'man' laid foolishly there.
How do we cross this concrete sea?
Said the badger to the foxes
With care and fear
Or you're killed by 'man's'
Metal speeding boxes.
Where have all the trees gone?
Said the starling to the crow,
'Man' has chopped them down
Built houses and flats
Nothing will ever grow.
Where have all the hedgerows gone?
Said the hedgehog to the mole
'Man' has pulled them down
And left a gaping hole.
How do we survive?
Said the wildlife to their 'god'
'God' could only answer
That 'progress is man's job'.
Where has all the wildlife gone?
Said the son to his father,
'Man' hung his head in shame
But could not give an answer.

Lisa Dilloway

Bosun

Your tail is always wagging,
Brown eyes so bright and clear.
You're always pleased to see me,
So happy when I'm near.

Your spirit always lifts me,
If ever I feel down.
At your amazing antics,
It's impossible to frown.

Your toys are all around you,
Scattered on the floor,
A ball, a bone, which one to choose
And which ones to ignore?

The park it is your playground,
Each path you know so well.
The shrubs and trees your landmarks,
Each one a tale to tell.

Running across the grass now,
Ears flying in the breeze,
A squirrel to chase, a stick to find,
A friend to stalk and tease.

The garden is your territory,
When you dig holes I sigh,
Will you find that buried bone?
Around you soil flies.

Dreaming of the park now,
Nose twitching in your sleep,
The fire is warm, the cushion soft,
Your slumber safe and deep.

And now it's nearly bedtime,
A last walk down the lane,
It's cold and dark, but you're so glad,
I really can't complain.
I wouldn't be without you,
You're such a friend to me.
When I'm away I miss you,
With you I'd rather be.

Sue Lowe

The Old Barn Cat

The old barn cat is looking rather sore,
She must be twelve years old or more.
Not for her the warmth of a fireside,
She'd rather curl up in the bales and hide.
Two litters of kittens a year she has had
But not now, is that why she looks so sad?
She comes for her food but she looks rather thin,
She won't let me catch her though I can tickle her chin.
She could tackle a rat but now she's past that.
She sleeps all day long curled up in the sun
Poor old barn cat, you've had a good run.
I suppose one day she'll be missing
And her bright little eyes will be closed,
Here puss, just let me tickle your chin once more.

Olive Torkington

FREE BIRD

See the eagle soar
So high
How I wish like that
        eagle
I could fly.
Free and easy through
the sky.
No demands,
No rules to obey.
If only adult life
        could be that way.

Bernadette O'Reilly

My Dog Is Waiting

In a distant field my dog is waiting
Ready for a game of ball,
She nimbly dances through the daisies
Her wagging tail held high in joy.
Her barking calls me ever nearer
Until I sit and close my eyes,
For then my tired and weary body
With aching limbs and stiffened back,
Will be freed from pain and every care
And I will join her in the meadow,
On a summer's day that lasts forever,
Where we can play and be together,
Always happy, young and free.

Caroline Merrington

The Horse

Into this world, in field or stable,
I come as fast as I am able,
A foal just now, but soon to be,
As fine a sight as you will see,

To pull a plough, or maybe race,
Whatever task, I'll bravely face,
My size can vary, nose to tail,
I'm really big, if a Clydesdale,

But way down South in the Argentine,
I come in sizes small and fine,
If highly bred, with pedigree,
To buy me you'll pay quite a fee.

For many years a friend to man,
I let him ride me if he can,
I'll amble on, or gallop fast,
For just as long as he can last,

But if you're lucky you may find,
A cheaper breed, but just as kind,
If for a plough my life is meant,
I'll pull it straight with good, intent,

Or on a race course, running fast,
Never to let the others past,
Or just a pony on the beach,
Not too tall, so kids can reach,

But whether plough or pony ride,
Allow me please to keep my pride,
All in all I don't much mind,
As long as man to me is kind.

Brian P Carroll

An Unconditional Love

Proudly perched on the window chair,
He sulks as I drive away,
Sam begins his morning watch,
As on every working day,

He scans the streets tirelessly,
Awaiting my eventual return,
Salivating in anticipation,
Yes! Food is his big concern.

This faithful little friend of mine,
He knows my every move,
Shadowing me day and night,
As if his love to prove.

When all the bustling is over,
Time to settle in my chair,
He offers up a soft warm paw,
To remind me he's still there.

Shirley Ann Lewis

JACK

'Oh, *please*,' beg those eyes
Like chocolate-covered nuts.
'Just a tiny bit of chicken
To calm my grumbling guts.'

'No,' I say quite firmly
Trying to look at my plate
As the black nose starts to quiver;
The tongue to salivate.

'Oh, *please*,' says the whine,
'Give me a tiny bit.'
I try hard not to notice
As he goes from 'stand' to 'sit'.

At last I give in
Although he's getting porky,
You just try to resist
Such an adorable Yorkie!

Lynda Blagg

Dino

The clouds cast their shadows
Across the once sparkling beads
Darkening her days and stealing the life
Now her memories are all that she sees

The dull echoes drift further and further away
Like the tides, they come and go
Until one day the serenity closed around her
No more can she hear 'Dino, no!'

The spirit flickers, the spirit lives
But is trapped within an aching frame
And the open fields that hold her dreams
Bring her limping home in pain

In youth she challenged, protected, lived
To love and enjoy her kith
Now, in twilight, her wagging tail has slowed
And I cherish each day she live

I dedicate these few short lines
To Dino, my dog and my sole mate
So much more than a pet, a part of my life
For who, old age can't overtake

Paula Wright

My Garden

It all started now one winter time,
When there wasn't much food about.
And I went into my garden,
And put a few goodies out.
Now they're always in my garden,
My friends don't know their name.
To name would be impossible
For they all look just the same.
Sometimes some big ones pay a call
Some pigeons or a crow,
The pigeons they live local,
The crows, well I don't know.
This year I made them a bird bath,
It's made from my old dog's bed,
Not all of them like the water,
Some prefer loose dirt instead,
Now they're always waiting in the trees,
When I put out their food each day.
Some are getting quite friendly,
They fly down, and don't fly away.

J M James

Sally (Loyal Friend)
1983-1996

Yesterday she was so happy
She couldn't know it was the end
She spent her life being a companion,
A doggy, a pet but most of all a friend.
She entered our lives, she had a good run
But you just didn't know what has to come
The pain is forever but it comes and goes
It hurts a lot and the tears will flow
But in the end you'll eventually
See that she had to leave for her sake
And not for you or me.

Sandra Seed

A Dedication To Burty

My precious little pet,
Know that you, I'll ne'er forget,
You filled my life, so full of joy,
Oh how I miss you darling boy,
I miss your fuss when I come home,
The house is full, but I feel alone,
I miss the love you gave so free,
Without you here I'm a misery,
I miss your loyalty oh so strong,
To lose you love, what went wrong?
The last two years you suffered bad,
Your poor sore feet near drove you mad,
We tried all the treatments that we could,
'Til in the end, we knew we should,
Release you from your painful life,
Though to us it meant heartache and strife,
And now you're gone, there's a huge abyss,
As from our lives you're sorely missed,
So from here we send all our love,
To you sweet Burty in Heaven above.

L P Smith-Warren

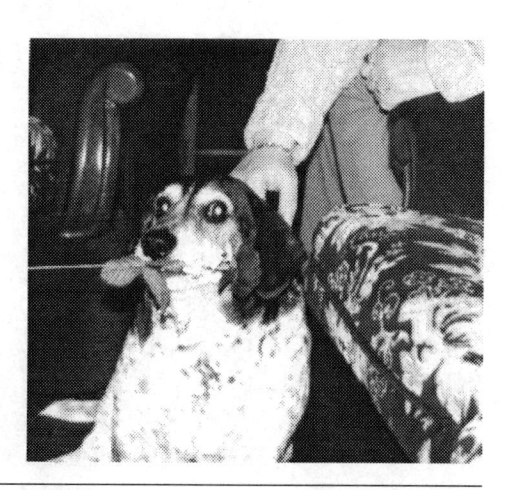

SAM

Far into the night
Across the woods
His fur did shine - a browny glow
Sam ran
Terror struck too soon
The fire soared
Thunder rumbled - rain fell
Fire burns
Sam scared
Clouds hurry across the sky
Sam afraid
Fire
Fire burns slowly
Red embers
Too hot
Deep in the woods
Trees die
Birds fly into smoky sky
Sam awakes
Nightmare over

In the garden
Sam, safe at last
No more fire
No more thunder

J M Stoles

Wise Owls

The owl they say is bright and wise,
But this to me is some surprise.
For all the owls I've known and seen,
Are really dim and not that keen.
Their eyes are bright and large and clear
Which makes them out to be austere.
Their hearing's sharp, their ears miss nowt,
But underneath as I've found out,
Their brains are small and neat and grey
Some do not like the light of day.
Their talons sharp and like a needle,
From 'neath the leaves a vole they'll wheedle.
They swoop and dive and hoot for fun,
Terrified, a rat may run.
The barn owl's white, the tawny brown,
The snowy wears a wedding gown,
The short-ear's eyes are brilliant yellow,
His cousin, long-ear an orange-eyed fellow,
Hides away from man and beast,
The tiny little owl enjoys a feast.
Every owl has charms its own,
Some hide away, then hunt alone.
Although their wisdom is unsure,
Each owl is welcome at my door.

Polly Pullar

CHLOE

She was brought back to the pet shop, three times in a row
The first ones said 'She bites the kids, so out she'll have to go'

The second, oh she'll squeal and shout,
We do not want her, throw her out.

The third, 'Oh well, she made some dust,
She laid an egg too' sheer disgust

I saw her every lunchtime, getting smaller and ragged and grey
Her eyes were closing, badly bullied, slowly fading away.

She had been kept in a budgie cage,
Squashed and cramped and bent

I could not stand it any longer
So home with me she went.

She does not bite, oh yes there's dust
She can shout a bit, but then she must!

She's now sleek and shiny, eyes bright and clear
She's joined the 'clan' and loves it here.

Those three who dumped her, have missed out so,
How we love her, our cockatiel Chloe
(nicknamed Clo Clo!)

Pam Bowyer

In Memory Of Misty

She wouldn't eat,
And she stopped drinking,
That hot summer of '93.
She lost too much weight
I watched her suffer,
She suffered too long.

No chance of recovery,
It's too late now.
All the suffering was over,
But she lived a long, happy, life.

Never seen my father cry like that before.
The guilt, I just couldn't cry!
Finally two weeks later,
The tears came flooding out,
I missed her so much!

Searching everywhere, her brother, didn't understand,
But as he realised, he became very upset and moped around the house.
They were very close!

The years go by,
But the sadness never stops,
It changes,
But it never stops.

Rosie Hart (14)

Companions, Lost

Timmy-Thomas liked to snooze
on our crumbling garden wall
in the warm setting sun
just waiting,
ears pricked, for me to say
or quite often hear me call -
with my washed hair in roller pins -
'TT, here is your din-dins'
which I know made his day
and mine
after all work was done.

                He regularly thought
                of that black and white Tom next door
                with its extended batch
                of sharp claws
                when tempers frayed or blew
                as happened many times before
                but Timmy-Thomas always won.
                I would shout 'TT, well done'
                and examine some new
                raw wounds
                to nurse bar the odd scratch.

He did not like to recall
that wood pigeon, all plump and fat
which pecked him on the nose,
I rescued
from his jaw and claws
'TT, they're too big - don't do that'
so he would try sparrows instead
and hide them under my bed
his curled up ginger paws
saying
'Innocent,' I suppose.

He became very friendly
with Esmie, the free-range rabbit
leading her to my back door
for tit-bits
and taught her sideways-slips
which became a funny habit
like sitting under my deck chair.
They made a splendid odd pair.
But now the sunset dips
alone
because they are no more.

Etelka Marcel

SCAMP

Hi, I'm Scamp, I was a tramp
Till these lovely people took me in.
They got me from a dogs' home,
(I think they liked my grin)
Well I have to say it made my day.
I'm well fed and they're nice to me too.
But I have this problem, I have to confess.
I've a terrible urge to *chew!*
They were kind when they came home to find
Their mat and their slippers in shreds.
But when it kept happening time and again,
They muttered and shook their heads.
They gave me a bone and a rubber gnome
But it didn't do the trick.
I pulled down the curtain and chewed that as well
- And it made me sick!
They did have a fit and their smiles slipped a bit
When I chewed through the wire to the telly,
But they only cried 'Oh, you could have been *killed!*
And they bought me a rubber welly!
They were still charming but it was alarming
When I overheard one of them say,
'We should take him back to the dogs' home.
'Oh, dear, oh dreadful day!'
What a fright but, it's all right.
'Mrs' told me so today.
Whatever I do and whatever I chew,
They'll *never* send me away.

Edna Ridge

My Mum

Would you believe it, I never would,
To see my Mum in front of me stood,
She's big and brown, with two clawed feet,
A pointed beak small and neat.
She scratches around, here and there,
Eating worms and other fare.
Then I take a look at me,
Something's wrong for I can see.
In the water, reflecting back, this very small
feathered bird,
But what I see is quite absurd.
I have a bill that's too big for me,
I'm yellow and fluffy, with two webbed feet.
So from where I stand, I'm not very neat.
Then my Mum comes up to me, I snuggle up
warm to be.
Why is it Mum we're not the same,
Please explain before I go insane.
Your Mum sat down on her egg,
Got fed up, wondered off instead.
So I jumped on to keep you warm,
And out you popped one spring morn.
That is when a dilemma arose.
For although I love you very much,
I cannot swim because I am not a duck.
But I will teach you all I can,
But when you swim, I can only hold your hand.

J Munday

Begging Your Pardon

The meat that went missing one Sunday?
Why, yes . . . I know what you mean,
But it wasn't my fault;
That dish on the table - the fragrance, temptation!
An excellent meal (though a bit too much salt),
Well, you've so often said, 'He's too lean.'

The curtains that somehow got damaged?
Oh, yes . . . but it's all in the past,
I've always maintained that you were to blame;
The bunching and pleating - I couldn't see out!
A twitch and a jump and *whoops!* . . . down they came!
Well, you said they were cheap, wouldn't last.

The holes that appeared in the garden?
Ah, yes . . . it was one of those nights,
Really an honest and simple mistake;
One can't be too careful when hiding possessions,
You filled in the lawn and trod on the rake,
Well, I saw it as one of my rights.

The slippers that got a bit shredded?
Oh, dear . . . a regrettable lapse,
A trivial and totally meaningless error;
The pounce and the fling - the rapture, excitement!
Well, we differ in notions of pleasure.

You think that perhaps I don't care?
Oh, please - my devotion's complete,
Some of my joys you may not comprehend
But loving is there and although I can't speak,

My tail always tells you that when our eyes meet,
I'm your funny, old canine companion! . . . and friend.

Adrian Cooper

A Hedgehog's Fear

He shuffled along the road,
Keeping to his hedgehog code.
He listened for the slightest sound,
In every hope not to be found.
His hedgehog friends were all long gone,
He was the only one that shone.
He lived his life with many a fear,
His future seemed so unclear.
With cars rushing past him at every minute
he felt his time was very near,
That he could only fear.
He longed for a friend and fun,
Even if there was no other sun.
As days passed by,
He felt he could only sigh.
'Where has my life gone?' he thought in his mind,
If only he could have some special find.
But then one day another hedgehog shuffled along the ground,
And at last what had he found?
The kind old hedgehog that longed for a life was
lying so still on the ground.

Kim Adams (11)

Fatal Attraction

As the evening dusk draws near,
and the daylight disappear.
The night begins to softly sing,
until you come, on gossamer wing.

You fly with ease, and make no sound,
as you float above the ground.
Your body small, it takes delight
in searching out the brightest light.

A candle burns - its flame so tall,
with dancing shadows on the wall.
Its golden centre calls with glee
as the candle flirts 'come play with me'.

You whirl around the candle flame,
in circles, round and round again.
The candle seems to hold you still,
as you spin and dance at will.

The candle's magic draws you in,
and so; with one last, dramatic spin
you touch its ecstasy. And you die,
as the candle flickers its last goodbye.

Frances Le Gray

The Scorpion

A falling star I feel the skies
Release me from my mother's sighs.
Governed by Pluto, he will see
I never shall a ruler be.
Yet, in his wisdom power give
To build great happiness herewith,
Or to destroy volcano like
With force of energy to strike.
How can I tell? Ah, I should know
For I was born a Scorpio.
I know my dreams will manifest
If wisely used at my behest.
Fiercely loyal to kith and kin
I raise my tail to plant my sting.
How can I tell? Yes, I should know
For I was born a Scorpio.

Monica F James

The Pekingese

Have you ever known a peke?
If not you've really missed a treat.
You have to know one really well
To learn the truth of what I tell.

Clever and proud is the Pekingese,
In old China - pet of the Empress,
He carried the hem of her dress with his teeth
And silently walked with hair on his feet.

He'd sit up and beg and stay there for hours
To amuse the Empress whenever she chose.
Mandarins carried him wrapped in their sleeves
And fed him on sponge cakes, eggs and cheese.

These proud little dogs know they are royal,
Your tiny companion will always be loyal,
You are his Empress, so treat him right
And all his life he'll be your delight.

Angela Kellie

Our Dumb Friend

We never have to tell him anything
Because he always knows
We never need apologise
But he always knows

Whether we are rich, whether we are poor
We never need explain
He trots beside us in the rain
And loves us just the same

He looks at us with his toffee-treacle eyes
To please us he always, always tries
Loving us all, he is so wise
Reading our thoughts 'Well he can't tell lies'

Clare Graham

Gem

For almost twelve years she was our friend
Loyal and devoted until the end.
Her original owner moved away
And she started to follow us one day.
Although a new home she had been found,
She returned again to familiar ground,
Outside the empty flat she sat
And neighbours fed her with this and that.
One asked if we could give her a home
As winter was coming and she shouldn't roam.

We did just that and it's a fact
Were amply rewarded for that small act.
Affection, amusement and slavery came too,
As a cat soon establishes who is who!
She soon got us into her routine
There was never a doubt that she was queen
The neighbourhood felines respected her too.
Keeping their distance if she should mew
Visitors were welcomed if they had a meal
Of meat and fish she would cadge her fill
Our lives were enriched by having her there
And being allowed her life to share
Never will she forgotten be
Living on in our memory.

Margherita Osborne

The Dinner Date

Hey you, you greedy pigeon
she threw that bread to me
they come to feed the ducks
not every bird they see.

I'm just as hungry as you are
I like bread and bacon rind
It makes a lovely change
from the scraps I usually find.

I never saw it quite like that
now I feel bad
there will always be someone to feed us
so please don't feel sad,

So let us be friends
whatever succumbs
share with me your bread and bacon
I will share with you my crumbs.

Julie D Ashton

Twinkle

I bought you from a pet shop and I thought you timid, shy.
I cuddled you and stroked your ears and hoped that, by and by,
You'd realise I loved you and your new life would enjoy.
I named you 'Twinkle.' You were like a furry, bright-eyed toy.
I knew you'd never get bad-tempered, never scratch or bite
And never, in your wildest dreams, would you begin a fight.

Within two months you'd used your claws and sharpened
                                                        up your teeth
Upon the hand that fed you, and I thought I sensed beneath
That innocence in your bright eyes a mental aberration,
In time it proved to be so, upon closer observation.
I knew you were a rabbit, but *you* thought you were a dog!
When you were angry you would growl, then snort just like a hog.

With time you've mellowed for you know I love you, oh, so much.
You snort with pleasure when you see me, leap down from your hutch,
Then flatten out and close your eyes, all ready for a stroke,
But let another buck come near and up you go in smoke!
You snort with rage and roll your eyes, a truly fearsome sight.
You've got another name these days which seems so very right.
'The psychopath' - and yet I wouldn't change you, furry friend.
You're crazy as your owner, one who loves you without end.

Phyl Clarkson

Tiger

Was it really all those years ago
When we brought you in - out of the snow?
Icy paw prints small in the snow soon led
To your frozen nest under our shed.
Of your feline Mum there was no sign;
So we brought you in and soon you were mine.

Over the years you've brought in many a mouse.
A pressie for me - carried into our house.
We've seen you stalk many a bird
We've frightened it off (bet you think we're absurd!)
You love to sit on top of our tiles
Queen of all you survey - you could see for miles.

If we went for a walk, you'd follow our path.
Then await our return crouched there in the grass.
Is it really true you knew the sound of our car?
You'd dash home to greet us no matter how far!
Your coat once so glossy now has grown dull.
A small meal and your tum feels so full.

Your teeth not so sharp now - your eyes not so bright.
Your limbs a bit stiff - especially at night.
We mince up your food - it is easier to chew.
For 18 long years we've had pleasure from you.
My hair has gone grey now - you do not stray far.
Yet still you appear to welcome our car.

We care for you still now your limbs have grown old.
We treasure the day you came in from the cold.
Each day that we share we think how many more?
Days of sunshine and shadow - will we still hear you purr?

Will you sit on our path and welcome our car?
Or will your spirit mew a welcome when you are not there!

Nancy Webster

ARRIVAL PRESS

Information

We hope you have enjoyed reading this book - and that you will continue to enjoy it in the coming years.

If you like reading and writing poetry drop us a line, or give us a call, and we'll send you a free information pack.

Write to: Arrival Press Information
1-2 Wainman Road
Woodston
Peterborough
PE2 7BU
(01733) 230762